THE JOY OF

OTHER BOOKS BY GARY R. COLLINS

Search for Reality
Living in Peace
Our Society in Turmoil (edited)
Man in Transition
Effective Counseling
Fractured Personalities
Man in Motion
Overcoming Anxiety
The Christian Psychology of Paul Tournier
Coping with Christmas
It's OK to Be Single (edited)
Make More of Your Marriage (edited)
The Secrets of Our Sexuality (edited)
Facing the Future (edited)
Living and Growing Together (edited)
How to be a People Helper
People Helper Growthbook
*The Rebuilding of Psychology: An Integration of
    Psychology and Christianity*
You Can Profit from Stress
Family Talk
Helping People Grow (edited)
Christian Counseling

THE JOY OF Caring

Gary R. Collins

WORD BOOKS
PUBLISHER
4800 WEST WACO DRIVE
WACO, TEXAS
76703

Contents

83531

Acknowledgments

The author gratefully acknowledges the cooperation of the following publishers who have given permission to quote from the sources listed below:

Abingdon Press—For excerpts from William E. Hulme, *Dialogue in Despair,* copyright 1968.

Augsburg Publishing House—For excerpts from Vernon J. Bittner, *Make Your Illness Count,* copyright 1976.

Chosen Books—For excerpts from Corrie ten Boom with John and Elizabeth Sherrill, *The Hiding Place,* copyright 1971.

Dolphin Books (Doubleday Company)—For excerpts from Marshall Bryant Hodge, *Your Fear of Love,* copyright 1967.

Family Concern—For excerpts from "Affirmation on the Family," copyright 1975.

Fleming H. Revell—For excerpts from Joan Winmill Brown, *No Longer Alone,* copyright 1975; Louis H. Evans, *Creative Love,* copyright 1977; Francis A. Shaeffer, *How Should We Then Live?,* copyright 1976; and H. Norman Wright, *The Christian Use of Emotional Power,* copyright 1974.

Harper & Row Publishers—For excerpts from Dietrich Bonhoeffer, *Life Together,* copyright 1954; Morton T. Kelsey, *Healing and Christianity,* copyright 1973; and Sherwood Eliot Wirt, *The Social Conscience of the Evangelical,* copyright 1968.

Hawthorn Books—For excerpts from Lucille Lavender, *They Cry, Too!,* copyright 1976.

Macmillan Publishing Co.—For excerpts from C. S. Lewis, *The Problem of Pain,* copyright 1962.

Perennial Library—For excerpts from Milton Mayeroff, *On Caring,* copyright 1971.

Regal Books—For excerpts from W. Ross Foley, *You Can Win Over Weariness,* copyright 1978; and Gene A. Getz, *The Measure of a Family,* copyright 1976.

The Seabury Press—For excerpts from C. S. Lewis, *A Grief Observed,* copyright 1961.

The Westminster Press—For excerpts from Paul Tournier, *The Strong and the Weak,* copyright 1963.

Zondervan Publishing House—For excerpts from J. Dwight Pentecost, *The Joy of Living,* copyright 1973; and Philip Yancey, *Where Is God When It Hurts?,* copyright 1977.

Preface

Several years ago I was invited to speak at a writers' conference. As I sat down to prepare my talk I turned to the Bible and discovered that there is only one real comment in the Scriptures about the writing of books, and that isn't very encouraging.

"My son, be warned," we read in Ecclesiastes 12:12. "The writing of many books is endless, and excessive devotion to books is wearying to the body."

As a teacher and a writer, my life is steeped in books. There are books in nearly every room of our home and all of the family enjoys browsing in Christian and secular bookshops. But sometimes I feel that too much is being published—over 1,000 new books *every day* (not including pamphlets, booklets, government reports and periodicals).

Before producing another book, therefore, a writer should have some clear reasons for doing so. I was invited to write this book and did so because there is no popular level volume on caring currently available.

I would hope that this volume could accomplish two important purposes: First, this book is intended to stimulate and encourage people to care for one another. As our world has become increasingly complex, many of us have become more and more self-centered and we have forgotten to care. But we need each other, and for the Christian, the Bible commands that we meet each others' needs.

How do we do this? This leads to a second reason for this book. The following pages are designed to give specific guidelines on the practical ways in which we can care for one another. This, then, is a "how-to-do-it" book.

I am deeply grateful to several people who have helped in the production of this volume. Charles Wenger offered periodic and much appreciated encouragement, while Jean Sweemer and Marlene Terbush typed and retyped the manuscript, sometimes under the pressure of deadlines. Lawrence Tornquist read the manuscript carefully, made a number of valuable suggestions for revision, and prepared the study questions. In the midst of a crowded and demanding schedule, my wife Julie found the time to go over each paragraph and offer numerous observations. These did much to add whatever psychological, theological, and literary polish you will find in the following pages. Each of these people cared enough to help me and in so doing taught me much about the joy of caring.

GARY R. COLLINS

Part I
The Principles of Caring

1

The Joy of Caring

IT HAPPENED ALMOST twenty years ago, but I remember the details so clearly that I can still feel the pain.

It wasn't a major incident. It wasn't even a crisis—like losing a loved one or being hurt physically. But it *was* an experience of being alone in a place where nobody seemed to care.

As a child I had always wanted to visit Europe. England held a special fascination for me, and after graduating from college I was finally able to save enough money to buy a one-way ticket to Europe. In those days poor people traveled by boat and the rich went by plane. I went on a ship—and enjoyed the voyage tremendously.

It was raining when we docked in Liverpool, but my life was bright with excitement. When the train pulled into London a few hours later, I said goodbye to my traveling companions, boosted my suitcase into a British taxicab, and excitedly announced my destination: a student hostel near Russell Square.

Ushered into the room that was to be my home for the next few months, I suddenly felt an almost overpowering emptiness in the pit of my stomach. The room was cold and damp, the bed was lumpy, the upholstered chair was losing its stuffing, and chips of paint were peeling from the walls leaving large ugly bare spots of grayish plaster.

"What am I doing here?" I wondered, perhaps out loud. I had little money, no job, no way to retreat back home across the Atlantic, and (this is what really hurt) there was no one in all of London who knew me or cared about me.

In the months that followed I met many caring, gracious people. During those first few days, however, I was alone and terribly lonely. And I was convinced that there was no one around who could care.

Perhaps most of us have had similar experiences. We have felt the pain of separation, discouragement, physical illness, anxiety, confusion, or spiritual doubt, and we have wondered if anyone really cares.

Does Jesus Care?

When I was growing up in Canada our church hymnal contained a song which asked the question, "Does Jesus Care?" and then went on to answer: "Oh, yes, He cares, I know He cares."

It is easy to sing like that when we are in a comfortable church building surrounded by friends and not especially burdened with the pains or pressures of life. But what about those times when we hurt? Do we really believe that Jesus cares when we are lonely (as I was in London), when we are weary, doubting, overwhelmed by worry, struggling with inferiority, trying to make some important decision, short on money, concerned about a rebellious child or a disintegrating marriage, facing a paralyzing illness, or weighted down with grief? Does Jesus really care then?

Back in the early days of Bible history, Joseph spoke to his brothers, assuring them that although he was about to die, "God will surely take care of you" (Gen. 50:24). This idea that a faithful God cares for individual people is repeated again and again throughout the entire Bible. We are told to cast our burdens upon the Lord because he will sustain us (Ps. 55:22). We are assured that if we trust in the Lord, do not lean on our own understanding, but acknowledge him in all our ways, then he will direct our paths (Prov. 3:5, 6). That is true divine caring. Jesus told us not to worry about the difficulties and the pressures of life because God, who cares for the grass of the field and knows about the sparrows, cares even more about us (Matt. 6:25–34). We are instructed to cast all our anxiety upon him "because He cares" for individuals (1 Peter 5:7). The entire history of Israel is a monument to a caring God. In his life on earth Jesus radiated caring, and the early church clearly experienced God's caring even in the midst of stress and considerable persecution.

The most convincing evidence that God cares, however, came when he sent his son Jesus Christ to live in poverty on earth, to experience the pressures and temptations of being human, and eventually to die on the cross like a common criminal. Jesus Christ never sinned. He was guilty of no wrong-doing, but he died a painful death to pay for the sins of the world—because God loves us and cared.

Jesus died so that we could have eternal life in heaven and abundant life on earth (John 3:16, 10:10). But God has never forced us to believe this. He has never compelled anyone to follow Jesus Christ here on earth. He respects us and cares enough to give us the freedom even to reject him. The day will come, the Bible teaches, when those who reject him will be sent to spend eternity in a place of eternal punishment. Others, however, will spend eternity with him in heaven because on earth they believed that Jesus is Lord, that God raised him from the dead, and that he has forgiven our sins (Rom. 10:9). By sending his Son to die for us and to save us, God clearly showed that he cared and cares.

It should not be assumed, however, that God always cares by acting in spectacular, supernatural ways. Clearly he has the power to intervene directly and miraculously in human situations, and at times he has done this. More often, it seems, God's work, including caring, is accomplished through the faithful and dedicated activities of Christian men, women, and children who are used by God to accomplish his purposes. When we cast our burdens on the Lord, very often he sustains us through the loving actions of some other person whom God uses to care for the needy, encourage the downhearted, and sustain the weak.

Caring is a part of God's nature and surely it must be central in the life style of every person who seeks to follow God's Son, Jesus Christ.

The Meaning of Caring

What is caring? Caring is the showing of a deep and genuine concern about the welfare of another person. It means loving others as we love ourselves. It is a reaching out with our lives in ways that can help another to grow and to know that he or she is not alone in spite of the pressures and the tensions of life. Caring is more than liking, comforting, showing sympathy, or having an interest in what happens to another person. Caring involves a concern that spills over into loving, compassionate acts. When we care we try to understand another person, we try to respect and commit ourselves to another, and we risk being involved intimately.[1]

To care is to know about another person. Caring is more than good intentions or a desire to help. To care for someone we first must know about that person's situation, needs, resources, and ability to cope. At times the other person will tell us what he or she needs, but this doesn't always happen. People are sometimes afraid to admit that they have needs, and often even they don't really know how they could be helped. To care, therefore, we first must try to understand, and to see things from the other person's perspective. Only then can we offer specific help.

To care is to respect another person. When we see people in need it is easy to start giving advice, to criticize, or to talk about others in a manner which approaches gossip. It is easy to look down on the needy or to show an attitude which says, "Unlike you, I've got it all together—isn't it wonderful that I'm going to help you?" Caring avoids all of this. When we care we respect another person too much to possess, dominate, or manipulate. Instead, we spend time showing love, care, concern, and a willingness to bear burdens. We look for ways which will enable other persons to grow, even if such growth means that they will stop coming to us for help.

To care is to be devoted to another person. In his thought-provoking book, *On Caring,* Milton Mayeroff writes that

> devotion is essential to caring. . . . Devotion is not an element that may or may not be present, as if I might be said to care and *also* be devoted. When devotion breaks down, caring breaks down. . . . Such devotion expresses my entire person rather than simply the intellectual or emotional part of me. Devotion is shown by my being there . . . in a way that is the converse of holding back and ambivalence.[2]

Real caring, therefore, involves sincere commitment.

To care is to take risks with another person. It is not easy to care for other people. Caring takes time, energy, a great deal of patience, and sometimes money. When we care for people we risk being misunderstood, rebuffed, criticized, and occasionally even harmed physically. But for the Christian, failure to care or to help others is to ignore those Bible passages (especially in the Book of James) which emphasize that faith in Jesus Christ must lead to works of compassion. We cannot complain about our helplessness or inadequacy and use this as an excuse for not caring. We cannot give to overseas missions (important as that is) while we ignore the spiritual and personal needs of people in our own neighborhoods. We cannot be content to dismiss problems with simple explanations whenever we don't have all the answers or when issues are too complex to be solved easily. All of this would be inconsistent with the actions and teachings of Jesus who was honest about the depth of human suffering and who risked getting close to those in need, even though at times this led to criticism and rejection.

The Helper-Therapy Principle

It does not follow that something is unpleasant just because it is costly or risky. There is, as we shall see, real joy to be found in caring in spite of—perhaps because of—the costs involved.

Several years ago a sociologist wrote an article describing what he called the "helper-therapy principle." Briefly stated, this is the view that those who help are the ones who are helped the most.[3] Alcoholics Anonymous discovered this when people with drinking problems found that a most effective way for controlling their drinking was to reach out to help other people who had similar needs. The same principle applies in almost all of the help groups which have taken the country by storm within recent years.[4] When we help and care for other people, the one who cares is the person who benefits the most.

There are several reasons for this. When we care for another we often feel the satisfaction and self-esteem that comes from being useful. We are able to observe problems at a distance, and as a result we get a clearer perspective on our own life situation. In reaching out we often feel a greater degree of personal competence and self-worth as a result of making an impact on another person's life. Then, in caring for one another we learn much about human behavior and feelings.

Our main purpose in caring must not be to gain something for ourselves. We care because God commanded it, because the Holy Spirit motivates us to care, because there is real joy in caring, and because it is a natural part of being a Christian. Nevertheless, there are fringe benefits that come from helping others. When we reach out to care and help others, we help ourselves. In fact, caring for others is probably the best way to help ourselves.

I discovered this in a small way during those difficult few days in London many years ago. Shortly after my arrival the door opened and in walked a man who was to be my roommate. He had also come from abroad, and, like me, he was very lonely. Almost immediately I began orienting him to the place where we were living and to the city where we had come to study. I took him sight-seeing, showed him the little bit of London I had already come to know, and tried to make him feel comfortable. I'm not sure whether this helped, since he left within a couple of weeks and went back to his home in South America. By then, however, my whole perspective had changed. I was beginning to enjoy my time in England, and I suspect that change in my attitude largely came first because I had stopped worrying about my own situation and secondly because I had taken the time and effort to reach out to another lonely person who needed to experience caring.

Accepting Care from Others

Jesus once said that it is *more blessed* to give than to receive (Acts 20:35). I wonder if he would also agree that it is *easier* to give than to receive?

On several occasions our family has traveled overseas to participate in seminars and missionary conferences. On almost all of these trips we have been amazed to see how God has provided the necessary expenses, sometimes within hours before our departure.

A few years ago, for example, we had been invited to spend six weeks in the Orient but we didn't have enough money to go. To our amazement we began receiving gifts from some of the most unexpected places and from people who really didn't have very much money. I discovered, however, that it was difficult for me to accept $10 and $25 gifts from students who were struggling to make ends meet but who wanted to help with our ministry overseas. It took us a while to recognize that these people wanted to give and that by refusing their gifts and offers of help I would be depriving them of the joy of caring for our family needs.

I still have trouble receiving, and it is probable that many other people feel the same way. Our society emphasizes independence, rugged individualism, and self-sufficiency. We don't like to depend on others, and we find it difficult, or even frightening, to let people care for us. But surely it can be encouraging to know that other people respect us, love us, and are concerned enough to care. It is an act of humility, of trust, and of giving to let others care for us, especially in our times of need.

Of course, there is value in caring for ourselves, doing what we can to help ourselves grow. Such self-help is limited, however. God did not create us to be alone. The Scriptures are filled with instructions to support, help, encourage, and care for each other. But such caring is a two-way street. It involves a person who needs and accepts care as well as a person who sees the need and gives the care. It is difficult to help someone who does not want our assistance, and it is frustrating to others when we don't let them care for us in our needs. If we are serious about bearing one another's burdens (Gal. 6:2) and about caring for one another (1 Cor. 12:25), then we must be willing both to risk reaching out with care and to accept, with gratitude, the caring that other people bestow upon us.

The Joy of Caring

According to one dictionary definition, *joy* is an emotion of keen or lively pleasure; a great gladness or delight; a state of happiness, outward rejoicing, or festive gaiety. Within recent years the word joy has begun to appear frequently in psychological writings where authors seem to equate joy with fun.

For the Christian, however, joy takes on a different meaning. According to Vernon Grounds, joy is "the deep down exuberance which comes from God through His Spirit by faith in His Son, regardless of outward circumstances or interpersonal relationships. Joy is supernatural in its source and essence, a foretaste of the face-to-face communion with God that will be rapture forever."[5] Joy is a word used repeatedly in the Bible not merely as an emotion, but as a basic characteristic of the Christian, a divinely produced sense of security, and an inner well-being which results from a unique relationship with God. Jesus promised full joy to those who keep his commandments and who abide in a close relationship with him (John 15:10, 11). On numerous occasions the apostle Paul made mention of joy even when he was in the midst of difficult circumstances. In the Book of Philippians, for example, joy is a major theme and is mentioned repeatedly even though Paul wrote from jail.

Real joy is not dependent on the outward events in our lives. It is possible to be in the midst of great difficulties but to still be filled with joy. Indeed, it has been suggested that problems and joy often go together, and even Paul commented that joy can come in the midst of sufferings (Col. 1:24; Phil. 2:17). If joy only came when things were going well, most of us wouldn't be joyful very often or for very long, but that deep down sense of well-being which is real joy persists in spite of the trials of life.

Dwight Pentecost has written that Paul could experience joy, even in the midst of suffering, because of a fellowship that existed between him and other believers.

> Do you think Roman imprisonment and all that it entailed was an easy experience for Paul? Do you think Paul enjoyed being stoned, beaten, shipwrecked?
> But Paul was joyful in it. Why? Because the saints ministered to him, and Christ's comfort was channeled through the saints. God takes many of his children through experiences where they find Christ's comfort and help through the saints for a time of need. . . .
> When a need comes into our lives, the natural response is to bear it alone. We consider it a sign of weakness, either human or even spiritual weakness, to share that need with another saint so that he might be a channel of God's comfort and help and encouragement. Because we try to bear without the help of the members of the body, we miss God's comfort, God's strength, God's joy. We do not for a moment suggest that Christ is insufficient, but Christ's help often comes from saints in a time of need.[6]

Paul's joy abounded when he let other people minister to him in his need and when he, in turn, was able to care for others.

Caring, then, can be difficult, challenging, time-consuming, and often inconvenient. But caring is therapeutic for both the one who cares and the one cared for. And caring gives us a sense of deep inner satisfaction and joy which can never come to those whose lives are spent in the pursuit of self-centered pleasures. In the pages which follow, we will consider what it really means to experience the inner joy which blossoms in times of caring.

2

The Who of Caring

NOT LONG AGO I was standing in a large airport, waiting to check in and get my seat assignment before taking a flight. Near the ticket counter was a lady in a wheelchair talking to one of the flight attendants who reassured the passenger that she would be cared for throughout the entire flight. When she heard this the woman made a remark which jolted me: "How nice of you to care for me without my having to pay extra."

Isn't it strange that anyone would think about paying extra in order to receive the care and attention that was needed? Have we reached a place in our society where we expect that people only care when they are paid to do so? Surely this would have been inconceivable in the thinking of Jesus. Caring is something that must be given freely, with no strings attached.

The Characteristics of Caring

Several years ago, some researchers discovered that all good people-helpers are characterized not by a desire to get paid, but by warmth, genuineness, and an ability to understand.[1] Are there similar marks of a caring individual? Although there may be little research to answer this question, the following eight traits, all of which can be developed, would surely be included in any portrait of a caring person.[2] As you read the list, don't get the idea that we can't care unless we have all of these characteristics. Few people have all of these traits in abundance, but we can acquire them. As they develop, we become more and more effective in our caring.

1. *Love.* Practical, compassionate, sensitive, giving love is of prime importance if any kind of effective caring is to take place. Such love is patient and kind. It originates with God the Father, was shown most dramatically when he sent his Son to die for us, and ought to characterize everyone who loves God and follows Jesus Christ (1 John 4:7, 11).

Gordon Allport, a well-known Harvard psychologist and former president of the American Psychological Association, once wrote a book in which he maintained that the love described in the Bible is without doubt "the greatest psychotherapeutic agent." It is, he suggested, something that professional psychiatry cannot of itself create but something which Christians understand and can show better than anyone else.[3] Regretfully, Allport also noted that there is an "age-long failure of religion to turn doctrine into practice," and as a result, he concluded that the believers who talk about love often fail to show it.

Jesus once gave his followers the commandment "that you love one another, even as I have loved you." He continued: "By this all men will know that you are My disciples, if you have love one for another" (John 13:34, 35). Love has been called the mark of the Christian but it only comes in its purest form to those persons who have committed themselves to Jesus Christ and are willing to let God's Holy Spirit so control them that love becomes characteristic of their whole lives. If we are not loving, perhaps we have never committed our lives to Jesus Christ. If we have committed our lives to Christ and still are not loving, then something is wrong with us spiritually. We need to ask God to give us more compassion and then we need to follow this prayer by engaging in loving actions. Often the feelings of love and concern come *after* we have begun to do loving deeds.

Some people, however, commit their lives to Christ and sincerely want to be more loving, but they have what one writer has called a "fear of love."[4] Deep down each of us probably has a strong desire to be taken care of, sheltered, protected, and loved by another person, but to experience such love or to express it in return can be threatening. When people get to know us intimately, they begin to see our weaknesses and there is always the possibility that such knowledge will cause them to reject us. To protect ourselves from this rejection, we maintain our distance and subtly push away the very people who most want to love us.

There are many ways by which we push people away. Sometimes we "close people out" by refusing to communicate or by not spending time with them. Sometimes we show indifference (a manner which implies "I couldn't care less—what you do doesn't really matter to me at all"). At times we develop attitudes of superiority or inferiority which we use to convince ourselves that the other person is either not good enough for us or too good. At other times we just ignore others or find faults which we then can criticize. All of these tactics create distance and help us to avoid the risks of getting close to people. They also keep us from experiencing the love that we so desperately need.

On occasion, most of us push people away at least temporarily. Even if we don't do this, it is important to remember that many people *are* afraid of intimacy and these people may reject us whenever we try to reach out in loving actions.

True love, therefore, involves patience and acceptance, even when we are pushed away or feel like pushing others away. True love says that "even though you and I get angry, even though we sometimes feel hurt or irritated, even though we withdraw, push each other away, or are bored, we cannot escape the fact that we are deeply involved with each other in a caring relationship. That fact of love exists whatever is happening between us at the moment."[5] When two people know that they have this kind of relationship they are freer to express emotions openly, to disagree, to risk being vulnerable, and to accept care from each other.

Several years ago a popular song proclaimed that love means I never have to say "I'm sorry." This idea may have been acceptable in a song or a love story, but it is never true in real life. True love and true caring involve a willingness to admit mistakes and seek improvement in our lives and relationships. To love and to overcome the fear of love, we must care for others in practical ways and we must let other people love and care for us consistently, patiently, and for a long period of time.

In no place should this love be more clearly expressed than in the church. The local body of believers should be a community where Spirit-filled Christians are free to love one another without fear of being condemned or criticized. Regrettably, this doesn't happen often:

> Many people whose lives are deeply intertwined with a religious group find it difficult to experience and express love because they have a tendency to suppress or repress many of their feelings. . . . Religious groups, like people in general, have not understood their fear of intimacy. Without realizing it, they have encouraged emotional distance between people rather than the experience of love they professed to promote. . . .
>
> In an effort to promote "fellowship" many congregations have coffee hours after church services. A typical remoteness and lack of self-revelation that usually marks these functions makes them even less productive of the experience of love than the average cocktail party, where people sometimes feel relatively free to be themselves and express some of their genuine feelings.
>
> Churches form study groups, women's groups, men's clubs, and couples' organizations. Although these groups talk about love and fellowship, they usually speak in very rational and impersonal ways. Such groups tend to become very uncomfortable and quickly change the subject if anyone begins to express deeply personal feelings about the subject under discussion. . . .
>
> Another way in which the church often promotes emotional distance is that it discourages honesty within its community. This happens because the church's preoccupation with behavior fosters the impression among its adherents that they will be condemned rather than accepted and loved if they are themselves. . . .
>
> The church has a rather poor record in helping people

experience the love of which so much is spoken. Despite lip service to the primacy of love in human relationships, the church, by and large, tends in practice to see moral value primarily in terms of external behavior rather than in terms of the experience of love. As a result of this approach, religious groups often appear to be concerned primarily with judging people.[6]

Although this is strong language which probably over-states the weaknesses of the church, these words do contain an element of truth. In our churches (and in our families) we could and should be more loving. Love is a rock bottom requirement for any kind of effective caring.

2. *Patience.* Patience implies endurance, persistence, and sticking with a person or situation even when no change seems to be taking place. Perhaps at no time or place in history has patience been a greater problem than in twen-tieth-century America where we have what someone has called "a fast food mentality." We are accustomed to instant puddings, fast hamburgers, minute steaks, and quickie pizzas. We want fast solutions to our problems, foreign language courses which promise fluency almost overnight, and even quick divorces. It is hardly surprising that many Christians have begun to look for sure and fast formulas for spiritual growth while failing to realize that things which grow quickly often wither and die under the pressures and storms of life. Frequently we expect people to change immediately and feel they are incompetent or failures if the process of change is slower than we would like. Too often, we become impatient when we think God isn't working quickly enough, we jump to conclusions and take matters into our own hands whenever difficulties arise, and we have trouble tolerating the weaknesses and lack of growth that we see in other people.

In contrast, the caring person is a patient person who stays with the one in need giving him or her time to grow and to think without feeling pressured to act or to make decisions quickly. The caring person does not look for fast change in the life of another, but patiently meets needs and expects that healing will come in due time.

Like love, real patience comes from God. It is listed as one of the fruits of the Spirit (Gal. 5:22) which comes to those believers who ask the Holy Spirit to fill and control their lives. Patience is not something which comes quickly. It is easy to pray, "Lord, give me patience and give it to me quickly," but God more often gives us patience by letting us wait in an attitude of expectant trust, while he works in accordance with his divine time plan.

Real patience is especially likely to come in the midst of trials and difficulties. Such experiences not only produce patience, they make us more mature, complete, and fulfilled (James 1:2–5).

Patience is a crucial part of caring. If we are to be caring people, we must be patient with ourselves so that we can learn to be patient with each other.

3. *Openness and honesty.* Let us suppose that you were not feeling well and decided to go to the doctor but that you refused to tell the physician how you felt or what was wrong. To say the least, the doctor would have difficulty in helping you because of your refusal to be open and honest about your symptoms.

Perhaps this is rare in medical clinics but it happens all the time in the offices of counselors. People are not honest about their real feelings, and sometimes, because of embarrassment or other reasons, they hide what is really bothering them.

Maybe, in our society, we are trained to hide our feelings. Little children are told not to cry, not to be angry, or not to hurt. As a result we learn to stifle our emotions and sometimes can't express our feelings or describe them in words even when we want to do so.

In caring for other people we must recognize this reluctance to express feelings, and we must gently encourage people to openly and honestly share some of their emotions and thoughts.

But how can we encourage other people to be open and honest? Perhaps the best way is for the carer to demonstrate this openness in his or her own words and behavior. Caring people should honestly try to see their own strengths and weaknesses, should seek to develop a genuine concern about others, and should show a willingness to accept other persons regardless of their behavior, beliefs, words, or attitudes.

It has been suggested that many counselors suffer from something called the "Yavis" syndrome.[7] They prefer to counsel those who are *Young*, *Attractive*, *Verbal*, *Intelligent*, and *Successful*. Such individuals are pleasant to work with, easy to accept, and likely to get better when they go for counseling. But most people don't fit into these categories, and in caring we sometimes must spend long hours with those who are hard to get along with, unattractive, and inclined to push us away. Remember that such persons need to be cared for too! All of us need caring friends who are authentic (not phony), genuine, honest about their own struggles and needs, willing to speak the truth in love and people who, by their example, encourage others to be honest and open in return.

Someone once said,

> Don't ask me to walk in front of you
> because I may not be a leader.
> Don't ask me to walk behind you
> because I may not be a very good follower.
> But invite me to walk alongside of you
> so we can learn together.

Honest, open, mutual burden-bearing involves walking alongside one another, encouraging, supporting, correcting, teaching, and gently confronting each other. Such openness and honest sharing is an important characteristic of healthy caring.

4. *Trust.* Think for a minute of people who have really helped you. It is likely that such persons accepted you, believed in you, and had confidence in your ability to grow and to mature even when you had no confidence in yourself. When people trust us like that we know that they care and this can help strengthen our self-esteem.

Do you remember the first time you learned to ride a two-wheel bicycle? When I was a kid, my father jogged up and down the street behind me holding on to the seat with one hand. Before long, and without my knowing it, he let go but continued to jog along ready to grab the bicycle in case I started to fall. Then one day, to my surprise, I found that he had stopped jogging and was watching, probably with a mixture of pride and nervousness, as I pedaled on down the street all by myself.

Perhaps this is a good way to picture what we do in caring. We come alongside for a while and hold the other person up. Then eventually, slowly, we let go, recognizing that in doing so the other person can be trusted to learn, even though he or she risks being hurt in the process.

Have you ever noticed that this is how God trusts us? He who is the Supreme Carer did not make us robots. He gave us the freedom to make choices and to rebel even against him. When we rebelled he accepted us and sent his Son to pay for our sins. Continually he forgives us (1 John 1:9), and goes on accepting and trusting us.

But he also expects us to trust in the Lord and not depend on our own understanding. Then, we read in Proverbs 3:5, 6 that if we acknowledge him in all our ways he will make our paths straight, showing us which way to go when decisions are pending. A similar challenge and promise is given in the thirty-seventh Psalm (vv. 3–7):

> Trust in the Lord and do good. . . .
> Delight yourself in the Lord;
> And He will give you the desires of your heart.
> Commit your way to the Lord,
> Trust also in Him, and He will do it. . . .
> Rest in the Lord and wait patiently for Him.

God expects us to trust him and in so doing we are freed to trust one another. Trust and care go together. Without trust we can't care, and it is only when we care that we can really trust.

5. *Hope.* Can you imagine how difficult it would be to care for someone if you couldn't offer any hope? Hope

involves a desire for something we want but do not yet have. When we hope, we yearn for something valuable, something that we cannot obtain by our own strength or resources, something which possibly could come but which also may not come. Hope brings comfort and at least temporary relief from suffering. It mobilizes our energy and enables us to keep on going even in the midst of difficulties. According to psychological research, hope comes and persists when we see or read about encouraging things that have happened to other people, when we have experiences in our own lives which give us reason to hope, and when we get information (from the Bible or from the doctor, for example) which leads us to keep on hoping. In all of this, other people are very important. If one's pastor, one's doctor, or (most important of all) one's family and closest friends lose hope, it is difficult for a person in need to keep on hoping.[8]

For the Christian, hope always involves an element of faith in that one expects help to come from God. Hope permeates the entire Christian message. It shines forth repeatedly from the pages of God's Word and is built, not on wishful thinking or on unfounded expectations, but on the assurance that God who created us is alive, always loving, and concerned about our needs even when all other reason for hope is gone. We may not sense his presence, but he is always there. He is all knowing, all powerful, and able to intervene in human lives.

Christian hope does not encourage people to deny the reality of their situations, to slip into inactivity, or to engage in perpetual wishful thinking. Christian hope rejoices in God's sovereign wisdom, accepts the fact that God's timing and ways of doing things are perfect, seeks for God's leading, learns to say, "Father, thy will be done," and accepts the fact that God's ways are not always our ways. It is not easy to think like this, especially when we are under pressure, but true hope assumes that some future event or some person will ease our present problems. For the Christian, that person is God who has promised to never leave or forsake us and is committed to provide for us in the future. Caring people point others to this God who is our only true and certain hope.

6. *Flexibility.* It is difficult if not impossible to care for people if we are rigid, unwilling to change, resistant to growth, or inclined to fit people into neat little categories. In any kind of caring relationship there should be a willingness to treat others as unique individuals. There should be a desire for growth both on the part of the carer and the one who receives the care. Growth implies flexibility and a willingness to both change and learn.

7. *Humility.* No one wants to be helped by someone who isn't really involved and who looks down on us from a "holier-than-thou" perspective. The person who cares is sincerely humble, not pretentious, willing to learn, reluctant to impinge on the privacy of others, and in no way inclined to present a "look-what-I'm-doing-for-you" attitude.

It is no accident that Jesus, the most compassionate man who walked on this earth, was also the humblest. In Romans 12, a chapter which is filled with practical instructions for caring, we are urged to present ourselves completely to God, to find his perfect will, and then not to think more highly of ourselves than we ought to think. It is then, humbly yielded to God and developing the gifts and abilities which he has given, that we are able to serve, love, do good, contribute, help, and care for one another.

8. *Self-understanding and self-acceptance.* Perhaps this surprises you, but how can we care for another person when we don't really respect and care for ourselves? How can we truly understand another person if we have no understanding or appreciation for our own needs, problems, hopes, fears, and motives?

Self-understanding and self-acceptance are difficult, of course, and never complete. Study of the Scriptures helps us to see ourselves as God sees us. Taking the time to ponder our own strengths and weaknesses can also be helpful. Have you ever done that? In addition, we must learn from the perspective of others who are willing to share their observations about us in a spirit of honesty and love. When someone else cares enough to help with our self-understanding and self-acceptance, we in turn become better able to understand and accept other people.

At this point you may feel that the above paragraphs present a list of caring characteristics impossible to achieve. It is important to emphasize once again that none of us ever "arrives" completely in all of these areas. And it does not follow that we must possess each of these traits in a fully developed form before we can care. Caring is a growing experience. As we care, these traits develop; as these traits develop we are better able to care. We do not wait for these traits to develop and then start caring. With God's help we reach out to other people in acts of compassion and concern, trusting that as we reach out God will help us to develop the attributes that will, in turn, make us more caring and compassionate Christians.

The Limits of Caring

When we become Christians each one of us is given a gift or gifts that come from God and are used for strengthening and building up the body of believers (Eph. 4:7–16). Although some people are especially gifted in the area of serving or showing compassion, all of us have at least some responsibility to engage in acts of compassion and love.

But can we care too much? Is it possible to be so concerned about others and so sensitive to their needs that the caring person has no time to rest, is dominated by needy people, and forgets his or her own family?

It is good to remember that no one person can care for everybody. God has given us families and close friends on whom we must put our prime caring emphasis. The Bible instructs us to care for all people, but we are to be especially concerned about fellow believers—those who are of the household of the faith (Gal. 6:10). Our own health, energies, time, abilities, and other responsibilities dictate that we must put some limits on our caring. We should ask

God to lead us to the people for whom he wants us to care most deeply. These may not be individuals with the "Yavis" characteristics—although it is important to remember that these people need caring too.

Is it possible to care too intimately? Caring, as we have said, involves closeness and the sharing of our lives. Sometimes it involves talking about personal problems, sexual issues, and deeply felt needs. The caring person must be alert lest he or she make caring an excuse for sexual intimacies and other personal liberties which are designed to meet the carer's own needs and are inconsistent with God's standards of purity as outlined in the Bible. Perhaps thousands of professional counselors and compassionate pastors have had their ministries ruined because they allowed themselves to become too intimate with people in need and failed to recognize that caring can make us especially vulnerable to our own sinful tendencies and fantasies. The same Holy Spirit who motivates us to care can also protect us from immorality if we are willing to commit ourselves to his control and protection.

Can we care for the wrong motives? There are times, perhaps, when all of us care because we have a sense of guilt—like the father who buys expensive gifts for his children because he feels guilty about his lack of personal involvement with the family. We may think we can cover some sin or failure by caring for other people, but we never deal with sin by hiding it or distracting ourselves (and others) from its presence. Sin is dealt with by confession, by asking God's forgiveness, and by accepting his cleansing, so that we are freed to care—because we want to and not because we feel guilty.

There are also times when we care in an attempt to manipulate others—trying to impress someone or to motivate another person to care for us in return. True caring, as we have said, is a two-way relationship. Whenever we care for someone we benefit and receive in return. But if caring exists primarily to manipulate other people we will find that our caring isn't very effective. People soon sense that they are being used, and they resist such manipulation. The best way to deal with others is not to manipulate them but to openly share our needs and concerns with them.

I have thought a lot about caring since I heard that comment by the lady in the wheelchair at the airport ticket counter. With God's help we can develop caring characteristics and learn to care "for free" without expecting others to pay for our caring. It won't be easy but it will be satisfying and a source of joy. Clearly such caring is a responsibility for everyone who follows Jesus Christ.

3

The Where of Caring

THERE ARE MANY things in this life that we can do alone. We can read by ourselves, play the piano with no one else around, eat by ourselves, and engage in a number of hobbies or athletic activities without anyone else being present. But we can't build a successful marriage by ourselves, it's pretty difficult to play football without a team, and we cannot care for others all by ourselves. Caring involves at least two people and has its greatest effectiveness when the carer is part of a compassionate, sensitive, supportive community of other caring persons. In our whole society perhaps there is no institution which has greater potential for caring than the local church.

I grew up in the church. My parents took me to church when I was far too young to understand what was happening there. I went to Sunday school, was actively involved in youth group during my teenage years, and even worshiped regularly during those days of college when almost all of my fellow students had rejected the church as part of their postadolescent rebellion. After completing graduate school I went to seminary, was active in the local church (where my wife and I were married), and taught first at a Christian college and later in a theological seminary where we heard much about the importance of the local body of believers. A few years ago, however, I faced up to the fact that I was very unimpressed with most of the churches that I had seen. I began to acknowledge that the local church has a lot of problems, problems which I had previously tried to overlook.

There was, for example, the issue of phoniness. People sang hymns and prayed piously on Sunday but never mentioned the Lord at other times. People took pride in the fact that they didn't drink, smoke, cheat on their income tax, or get angry—nevertheless they could be gossips, unkind, and unable to get along with others. I began to wonder if anyone in church experienced the temptations, anger, lust, prejudice, criticism, and depression which were more a part of my life than I wanted to acknowledge but which rarely were acknowledged in the local body of believers. I began to think of the church as a place where there was no intellectual challenge, no willingness to change, no talk about real problems, and very little commitment in the lives of the people. Instead, it appeared to be a place where "fellowship" consisted of superficial chatter over coffee and where few people really cared in spite of much talk to the contrary.

These doubts about the church came after I was well established as a professor in seminary, concerned about the spiritual needs of my students, and alert to the spiritual development of my family. For a while I thought about quitting the church and not attending for a period, but what would I have said to my children or to my students? It also would have violated the clear biblical teaching that Jesus Christ, who founded the church, expects us as Christians to assemble together regularly for worship, fellowship, teaching, and prayer—whether or not we like it or find phoniness in the body.

After a period of struggle, I began to see what generations have acknowledged before me: the church is not perfect. It is not a body of mature, problem-free people but neither is it as bad as some of its critics claim. It is, as someone has said, a hospital for sinners and was never intended to be a museum of saints.

The tenth chapter of Hebrews includes some reassuring words for times when we are inclined to give up on the church.

> Since therefore, brethren, we have confidence to enter the holy place by the blood of Jesus, by a new and living way which He inaugurated for us through the veil, that is, His flesh, and since we have a great priest over the house of God, let us draw near with a sincere heart in full assurance of faith, having our hearts sprinkled clean from an evil conscience and our body washed with pure water.
>
> Let us hold fast the confession of our hope without wavering, for He who promised is faithful; and let us consider how to stimulate one another to love and good deeds, not forsaking our own assembling together, as is the habit of some but encouraging one another; and all the more, as you see the day drawing near (Heb. 10:19–25).

This passage begins with a reminder that we who are followers of Jesus Christ have been cleansed because of his blood. Now we have the privilege, through prayer, of coming into the presence of God the Father. Because of this there are certain things we can do:

–We can draw near to God with no fear and with absolute confidence that he accepts us.

–We can hold fast to our faith without wavering because we know that God is faithful and will make good on all of his promises.

–We can consider how to stimulate one another to love and good deeds.

–We can meet together with fellow believers, not forsaking our assembling together as is the habit of some, but encouraging one another and caring for one another as the day of Christ's return comes closer and closer.

In the midst of my struggles with the church that passage in Hebrews helped me to see that meeting together with other Christians should not be something which we do out of habit or because it is some grudging duty. We meet together to pray, to worship, and to remind each other of what God has done for us and of the hope that we have in Jesus Christ. We must meet together to encourage one another and to stimulate each other to love and good deeds.

A friend of mine expressed this beautifully one Sunday afternoon when we were having dinner at his home.

"There are a lot of hurting people in my church," he said. "There are also a lot of attitudes and actions which I don't like. Nevertheless, I recognize that nobody in the church is perfect, including me. So I jump in to do what I can with the skills and gifts that I have. I try to minister to other people who might be hurting like me."

My attitude toward the church has changed. I no longer sit around waiting for other people to care and neither do I criticize when such caring is not forthcoming. Instead, especially by my actions, I try to stimulate love and good deeds in the church and to encourage other believers. If each of us would take the responsibility of reaching out to our fellow believers in a loving way, then the church could become the caring community it was meant to be, and the people around us would begin to know that we are Christians because of our love.

Caring and the Church

Several years ago I read someone's thought-provoking description of what much modern religion is like. It:

> –talks about God but avoids mention of anything contro-versial like sin, the virgin birth, and the reality of miracles, or the authority of the Bible;
> –emphasizes love, hope, good will, togetherness, success-ful living, and practical achievement, but says nothing about repentance, self-denial, the costs of commitment, or the holiness and wrath of God;
> –is tolerant of all people and thus avoids evangelism or reference to a Christian life which is separate from the world's values; and
> –assumes that the basis of religion is not the right beliefs but right action.

Hopefully this doesn't describe your church (or does it?). This is a widely accepted but dangerous view of religion. It really is a form of atheism preached from many contemporary pulpits in so subtle a way that thousands of people who attend church and attempt to live a good life nevertheless fail to see their need for a Savior or the costs of discipleship.

This is far removed from the Great Commission that Jesus gave to his followers before ascending into heaven after the resurrection. "All authority has been given to Me in heaven and on earth," he said. "Go therefore and make disciples of all the nations, baptizing them in the name of the Father and the Son and the Holy Spirit, teaching them to observe all that I commanded you; and lo, I am with you always, even to the end of the age" (Matt. 28:18–20).

Modern forms of religion also tend to overlook the great commandments that Jesus gave: "'You shall love the Lord your God with all your heart, and with all your soul, and with all your mind.' This is the great and foremost commandment. And a second is like it, 'You shall love your neighbor as yourself'" (Matt. 22:37–39). The Great Commission and the great commandments together are our marching orders for the church. When we obey these orders, we experience a deep joy and often see a lively church—but we are also likely to see criticism, hardship, and even persecution. Jesus experienced such difficulties, and he warned his followers to expect the same.

Christianity, therefore, is not some game that we play to amuse ourselves. It is not some easy "no-demand" kind of belief system to which people give half-hearted allegiance. The church is not a social club which exists for entertainment, relaxation, and an occasional charitable outreach. Christianity puts demands on believers and according to Lorne Sanny, president of the Navigators, the church of Jesus Christ must be involved in three major and significant tasks.[1]

1. *Evangelizing.* The main thrust of the Great Commission is that Christians should make disciples. Jesus taught that all people are sinners and in need of a Savior. He never maintained that we become Christians because of birth,

nationality, family membership, church attendance, or involvement in good works. Instead, he proclaimed that if any person wanted to have eternal life it was necessary to confess his or her sin to God, to believe that Jesus Christ could forgive, and to yield one's whole life to Christ's control. Furthermore, Jesus taught that his death was to pay the penalty for the sins of mankind, thus making it possible for anyone who wanted to do so to become a child of God.

The Great Commission instructed Christ's followers to proclaim this message, to urge others to put their faith in Christ, to baptize new believers, and to teach them the Scriptures. According to 1 Timothy 2:4 God wants all people to be saved and to come to a knowledge of the truth. But people can't find this truth and believe in Jesus Christ unless they have heard the message. And people can't hear the message unless there is someone to tell them (Rom. 10:13–15). Telling others about Christ is what we mean by evangelism. It is the responsibility of all Christians to evangelize by what we are, what we do, and what we say.

Evangelism and caring go together. Calling people to serve, love, and care for one another is an integral part of the gospel. This is seen throughout the Bible but nowhere more clearly than in 1 John 4:7–11.

> Beloved, let us love one another, for love is from God; and every one who loves is born of God and knows God. The one who does not love does not know God, for God is love. By this the love of God was manifested in us, that God has sent His only begotten Son into the world so that we might live through Him. In this is love, not that we loved God, but that He loved us and sent His Son to be the propitiation for our sins. Beloved, if God so loved us, we also ought to love one another.

2. *Establishing.* Once a person becomes a Christian there begins a long, slow process of growth toward Christian maturity.

Who is responsible for this growth? Is it God? Is it other Christians? Is it the believer? The answer is "all three." God is the one who establishes us in the faith (Rom. 16:25).

Fellow believers have a responsibility for teaching and counseling one another (Col. 3:16), and Christians must build themselves up in the faith (Jude 20).

According to Lorne Sanny[2] believers should ask themselves several questions:

—Am I surrendered to Christ and to his will for me?
—Is there daily obedience to the known will of God?
—Am I growing and becoming established in God's Word: hearing it preached, reading it daily, studying and memorizing it, meditating upon it to make it part of my spiritual bone and sinew?
—Am I growing in my practice of intercessory prayer and in my personal times of devotion with God?
—Am I seeing answers to prayer regularly?
—Do I take an active part in a warm church fellowship and in group Bible studies with those of like mind?
—Am I ready to share the Good News about Christ with someone who does not yet know him?

When all of these elements are present in a believer's life "it is a safe assumption that he (or she) is being established and maturing" in the faith.[3]

In the midst of a discussion about the church, the apostle Paul once outlined his real life purpose—a purpose which could very well be the life goal of every Christian: to proclaim Christ, admonishing and teaching everyone so that every person could be "complete in Christ" (Col. 1:28, 29). Helping people to mature as Christians is what we mean by the process of making disciples.

Elsewhere in his writings, Paul instructed young Timothy about the ways in which this discipling process should take place. He wrote, "My son, be strong in the grace that is in Christ Jesus. And the things which you have heard from me in the presence of many witnesses, these entrust to faithful men, who will be able to teach others also" (2 Tim. 2:1, 2). Here Paul was teaching Timothy, who in turn taught faithful men, who then could teach others. Helping people mature spiritually is one of the major purposes of the church. It also is one effective way by which we can care for people and help them, in turn, to care for others.

3. *Equipping.* In several passages of the New Testament we read about spiritual gifts—special abilities given to Christians by God to strengthen and build up the church. Each believer has received at least one special gift (1 Peter 4:10), and we have a responsibility to "employ it in serving one another, as [God's] stewards." Sometimes we fail to realize that Christians have both their natural abilities and their special gifts. Our gifts may lie dormant because we are unaware of their presence or are unwilling to use them. As disciples we should seek to discover and develop our gifts. This will get us involved in serving each other and "growing toward spiritual maturity."

When all of this is put together we see that the church as an evangelizing, establishing, equipping community will also be a community intent on fulfilling the Great Commission and actively obeying the great commandments. It will be a community which loves, worships, praises, obeys, and learns about God, and it will be a community which shows love not only to other believers within the body but to those who are in the community.

Caring in the Church

When I was having my struggles with the church I decided to see if I could find a caring church which met the biblical guidelines for the local body of believers. To my surprise, I discovered that there are many caring churches. They come in all sizes, in different localities, and in a variety of denominations.

One of the most impressive was a small group of believers who meet in a plain little house in a rundown section of an eastern U.S. city. One of the leaders of this body talked with me for a couple of hours about his church community.

"We see the church as an extension of the family," he said. "In church we find a support group with whom we can share, worship, learn, and get help in making decisions." My friend was not critical of big affluent churches, except in those situations where money and tradition provide security and substitute for warm sharing relationships with other people.

But can a large church show caring and concern to other people in the body? The answer clearly is yes. Consider, for example, the prestigious National Presbyterian Church in Washington, D.C. Many of the members are involved in what the pastor calls "covenant groups." The participants in these groups meet regularly to pray, study the Bible, and in a caring way share with one another in accordance with the eight principles listed in Table 1.[4]

Several years ago there developed an enthusiastic interest in something called "church renewal." Distressed by the lack of relevance, growth, and caring in many local churches, there was a surge of interest in how we could make the church more biblical, more meaningful, and more caring. As a result of this discussion church renewal has taken place in a variety of settings. What has worked in one church may not work in another, but any group of believers who takes the Great Commission and the great commandments seriously is well on the way to becoming a church where Christians can really learn to care for one another within the body.

Caring through the Church

It is no secret that we live in a society populated by people with a variety of needs. Loneliness, emptiness, family breakdowns, poverty, prejudice, violence, and a host of other problems make life difficult for millions of people. The church has responded to these needs in a variety of ways. Sometimes there has been an active involvement in social action almost to the exclusion of any spiritual ministry to those in need. At other times and in other churches, community needs are virtually forgotten on the assumption that preaching the gospel is the only responsibility we have in reaching out to the needy people around us.

Table 1

Principles of Covenant Groups

1. *The covenant of affirmation (unconditional love, agape love):* There is nothing you have done or will do that will make me stop loving you. I may not agree with your actions, but I will love you as a person and do all I can to hold you up in God's affirming love.
2. *The covenant of availability:* Anything I have—time, energy, insight, possessions—is at your disposal if you need it to the limit of my resources. I give these to you in a priority of covenant over other noncovenant demands. As part of this availability I pledge my time on a regular basis, whether in prayer or in an agreed-upon meeting time.
3. *The covenant of prayer:* I covenant to pray for you in some regular fashion, believing that our caring Father wishes his children to pray for one another and ask him for the blessings they need.
4. *The covenant of openness:* I promise to strive to become a more open person, disclosing my feelings, my struggles, my joys, and my hurts to you as well as I am able. The degree to which I do so implies that I cannot make it without you, that I trust you with my problems and my dreams, and that I need you. This is to affirm your worth to me as a person. In other words, I need you!
5. *The covenant of honesty:* I will try to mirror back to you what I am hearing you say and feel. If this means risking pain for either of us, I will trust our relationship enough to take that risk, realizing it is in "speaking the truth in love that we grow up in every way into Christ who is the head" *(see* Ephesians 4:15). I will try to express this honesty in a sensitive and controlled manner and to meter it, according to what I perceive the circumstances to be.
6. *The covenant of sensitivity:* Even as I desire to be known and understood by you, I covenant to be sensitive to you and to your needs to the best of my ability. I will try to hear you, see you, and feel where you are and to draw you out of the pit of discouragement or withdrawal.
7. *The covenant of confidentiality:* I will promise to keep whatever is shared within the confines of the group in order to provide the atmosphere of permission necessary for openness.
8. *The covenant of accountability:* I consider that the gifts God has given me for the common good should be liberated for your benefit. If I should discover areas of my life that are under bondage, hung up, or truncated by my own misdoings or by the scars inflicted by others, I will seek Christ's liberating power through his Holy Spirit and through my covenant partners so that I might give to you more of myself. I am accountable to you to become what God has designed me to be in his loving creation.

Jesus both preached the gospel and ministered in practical acts of compassion. Surely the church must do the same. We must present the Word of God *and* reach out to care. We must acknowledge that the gospel involves both words and an active involvement in the lives of those needy people who live both in our own neighborhoods and in the world beyond.

In a little book on caring Chester Custer once painted a picture of the caring church.[5] The following portrait is adapted from Custer's list.

1. The caring church consists of believers in Jesus Christ who submit to his Lordship and seek to live and worship in accordance with the teachings of the Bible. Caring church members are concerned about evangelizing, establishing disciples, and equipping believers so that they in turn can serve one another, present the gospel to others, and reach out in compassion to the community both at home and abroad.

2. The leadership of a caring church, including the pastor, consists of people who are seeking to grow as men and women of God and who show genuine warmth and concern for other persons. Genuine interest in persons is expressed through listening, encouraging, supporting, and guiding— all of which take place in an atmosphere of understanding and empathy.

3. Worship services develop a climate which is both Christ-centered and concerned with the needs of the worshipers. A real effort is put forth to make persons sense that they are welcome and a part of the worshiping community. The truths of the Scripture and the real needs of people in the congregations are kept in mind when the speaker prepares and delivers sermons or when he teaches. Opportunities are provided for the stating of prayer requests and for church members to express their personal concerns.

4. A program exists which enables members of the body to bear one another's burdens and minister to one another. Such programs permit the pastor and lay persons to engage

in a cooperative mutually supportive ministry. There is an outreach to persons who have recently moved to the community, to those who are ill or in special distress situations, to those without families, to the lonely, to the homebound, and to those in institutions. Individuals and groups in the church attempt to discover and meet the needs of persons in the congregations and the community.

5. Groups which meet for prayer, Bible study, or action outreach provide opportunities to share personal problems and feelings in an atmosphere of acceptance and Christian love. While not deviating from scriptural teaching, the church tries to relate creatively to persons with different theological views, religious experiences, and life styles.

6. Sunday school teachers who know about Christian education are also trained in the principles of good inter-personal relationships. They learn how the theological and experiential dimensions of faith go together, and they are able to show students how Jesus Christ can meet one's daily needs. There is a personal concern for students and a followup of absentees.

7. There is a deep concern for Christian missions and a desire to bring the gospel to people within the local community and in other parts of the world. There is concern both for the *saving* (evangelistic) and for the *social* (com-passionate) aspects of the gospel. The church shows a practical concern for the needs of mankind but also empha-sizes the loving message of salvation through faith in Jesus Christ.

8. Stewardship and service opportunities are provided by which persons can express their Christian commitment in tangible and practical ways.

9. Financial priorities are determined in accordance with the church's purposes as taught in Scripture. Funds are used in ways which support those purposes and meet human needs—both spiritual and physical.

10. The church attempts to fill leadership positions with individuals whose lives and words show that they are maturing disciples of Jesus Christ who also have a concern about caring.

Conclusion

In 1 Peter 2:5 the church is described as a building which consists of living stones and holy priests who offer up spiritual sacrifices to God.

Has it ever occurred to you that a brick by itself is pretty much useless? It only becomes of maximum value when it is combined with other bricks to produce a building. Individual Christians are like that. We find our true place as Christians when we are in the body integrated together with other believers to form a solid spiritual house.

But notice that each believer is also a priest. A priest is someone who has access to God, who brings others to God, and who offers spiritual sacrifices. We Christians no longer offer sacrifices of animal blood. Instead, we are to offer our own bodies and lives as living and holy sacrifices (Rom. 12:1). It pleases God when we praise him verbally (Heb. 13:15). It also pleases him when we offer a sacrifice of doing good and sharing. With such sacrifices God is well pleased (Heb. 13:16). This is what he wants from his church—the body where caring takes place.

4

The Why of Caring

JONI EARECKSON[1] WAS a teenager in 1967—pretty, popular, and athletic. She liked to ride horses, to bounce a basketball against the side of the family cottage, and to swim.

It was the swimming that created the problem. As she dove from a raft one day, into Chesapeake Bay, her head crashed into the bottom with a jolt.

"I couldn't move," she wrote later.

> My face was pressing against the grinding sand on the bottom, but I couldn't get up. My mind was directing my muscles to swim, but nothing responded. I held my breath, prayed, and waited, suspended face-down in the water.
>
> After maybe a minute I heard Kathy [her sister] calling me—a faint, muffled voice above the water surface. Her voice came closer and clearer, and then I saw her shadow right over me. "Did you dive in here? It's so shallow," I heard her say.
>
> Kathy reached down, tried to lift me, then stumbled. *Oh, God. How much longer,* I thought. Everything was going black.
>
> Just as I was about to faint, my head broke through the surface and I choked in a great gulp of air. I tried to hold on to Kathy, but again my muscles would not respond. She draped me over her shoulders and began paddling to shore. Sure that my hands and legs were tied together around my chest, with a sudden shock of horror I realized that my limbs were dangling motionless over her shoulder.[2]

Joni was rushed to Baltimore's city hospital, her brand new swimming suit was snipped off, her long flowing blond hair was shaved from her head, and as she began fading from consciousness she remembered someone holding her head while the doctor drilled a neat hole into either side of her skull.

Joni awoke to find herself strapped onto a metal frame. Paralyzed from her neck down, she was about to begin a long process of surgery, loneliness, anger, and struggles with the question "Why?"

Most of us who are healthy prefer to avoid people like Joni. In the presence of paralyzed, diseased, and suffering people we feel so helpless. Perhaps we feel guilty about our own good health or our own lack of involvement with needy people. Perhaps, at such times, we feel confused about what we should say or do. Then, for many people, suffering presents some theological questions which are difficult to answer. C. S. Lewis summarized these questions concisely in his book, *The Problem of Pain.*[3] If God is good, then why does he permit suffering? If he is all powerful, then why doesn't he do something to stop the hurt and bring about healing?

These questions were raised dramatically in a motion picture which portrayed the suffering of Corrie and Betsie ten Boom in a Nazi prison camp during the second World War. From her bunk in the crowded barracks, one little lady leaned over to the ten Boom sisters and announced that she had been the first violinist in a symphony orchestra. Stripping the bandages from her bony injured fingers she asked in a taunting manner: "Did your God allow this?" Then she went on to propose that the God of the ten Booms was either a sadist who didn't care or a powerless being who couldn't do anything about suffering.

Why does a compassionate loving God permit suffering? Why doesn't God do something to stop the hurt? Why does he let us become bitter, angry, discouraged, helpless, plagued by self-pity and doubting just when we need him most? In another one of his writings C. S. Lewis expressed these feelings poignantly:

When you are happy, so happy that you have no sense of needing Him, so happy that you are tempted to feel His claims upon you as an interruption, if you remember yourself and turn to Him with gratitude and praise him, you will be—or so it feels—welcomed with open arms. But go to Him when your need is desperate, when all other help is vain, and what do you find? A door slammed in your face, and the sound of bolting and double bolting on the inside. After that, silence. You may as well turn away. The longer you wait, the more emphatic the sounds will become. . . . Why is He so present a commander in our time of prosperity and so very absent a help in time of trouble?[4]

If we can avoid suffering we don't have to face difficult questions like these. But each of us does encounter suffering at times, and it isn't always possible to push the disturbing questions out of our minds. As a result, we sometimes scramble to find simplistic answers and then go on our way as if the problem of pain had been solved. Sometimes we hope for a miracle, and if the miracle doesn't come, we find some explanation that will "get God off the hook" and let us go on believing without our theology being threatened. In extreme cases, we become like a crippled lady who once explained that although she couldn't walk she nevertheless was healed already even though her legs "just don't believe it yet." Sometimes we assume that we "don't have enough faith" and go on our way thinking that if somehow we could believe more intensely, then healing surely would come.

All of these are mental games which we use to avoid the problem of suffering—a problem which, when faced honestly, can arouse doubts, nibble away at our self-confidence, and lead to inner fears, confusion, or discouragement. The presence of suffering raises important questions both about the nature of God and about our own place in the world. A willingness to struggle with these questions can lead to greater spiritual maturity and increased effectiveness in caring for others.

Why Do People Suffer?

For centuries, Christians have struggled with the problem of pain and the meaning of suffering. In their attempts to discover why we suffer, many Christians have concluded that God's ways are far too deep for our little brains to comprehend. Certainly we can only get a limited glimpse of the answers we seek. Nevertheless the Scriptures and our own reason do help us at least partially to understand why human beings suffer.

First, we suffer because we are part of the human race. Pain comes at times because we never exercise, don't eat properly, fail to take care of ourselves, or come into contact with some kind of a virus or disease. When this happens it is good to remember that God, who is omniscient, knows about everything we suffer. Nothing is permitted to happen without his awareness. We see this clearly in the Book of Job where Satan used his supernatural (but limited) powers to bring suffering into the life of Job, but only after God, in his wisdom, had permitted that to happen.

This brings us to a second reason for suffering: sin. When our ancestors first disobeyed God, sin entered the world, and with it pain and suffering became a part of the human condition. All hurting, ultimately comes because of mankind's sinful condition. But when an individual suffers, is this a result of his or her own deliberate sin? It would seem that pain sometimes does come because of sin in the sufferer's own life, but this isn't always true. We all know people who live in great sin without apparent suffering, and others, like Job, who live exemplary lives but still suffer.

In several places the Bible refutes the popular idea that suffering is always the result of the sufferer's own sin. In John 9, for example, the disciples asked Jesus about a man who had been born blind. Perhaps with an air of superiority they asked, "Who sinned, this man or his parents?" Jesus bluntly replied that neither had sinned and that God was not punishing this man or his family through illness, as the disciples had assumed. The same idea was expressed in Luke 13 where Jesus was told about some Galileans who apparently had died as part of a heathen sacrifice and about some men who had been killed when a tower fell on them at a place called Siloam. "Do you suppose that these Galileans were greater sinners than all other Galileans because they suffered this fate?" Jesus asked. "Do you suppose that those people on whom the tower in Siloam fell . . . were worse culprits than all the men who live in Jerusalem?" Jesus answered his own questions with a resounding "no!"

It cannot be assumed that tragedy, suffering, and pain are punishments that indicate God's displeasure with the sufferer. Sometimes, as with the ten plagues in Egypt, suffering does come as punishment. In other cases, as with Job, there is no reason to believe that God is punishing us through suffering or that he is trying to tell us something by bringing pain into our lives.

A third reason for suffering is that it helps us grow and mature. The apostle James told us to consider it all joy when we encounter various trials "knowing that the testing of your faith produces endurance." And that endurance helps to make us mature (James 1:2–4).

In 2 Corinthians 12:7–10 the apostle Paul makes reference to some kind of a personal problem, "a thorn in the flesh," which never left in spite of Paul's continued prayers for healing. Paul accepted this discomfort because it kept him from exalting himself. It taught him to depend on God and it showed that we human beings are strong only when we acknowledge our weaknesses and commit our lives to God.

Elsewhere in the New Testament we read that suffering refines our faith (1 Peter 1:5–7), conforms us to Christ's image (Rom. 8:28, 28), makes us more Christlike (Heb. 12:11), and produces both perseverance and character (Rom. 5:3–5). Psalm 119:71 shows how suffering teaches us about God.

At one time when things were particularly difficult in his

life, the prophet Jeremiah prayed for protection and God replied by sending the prophet to see a vessel being made on the potter's wheel. Jeremiah watched as the clay was pounded, torn apart, pushed back together, and eventually molded into a vessel of beauty which then was placed into a hot oven (Jer. 18). God does that to us (Rom. 9:20–21), molding us like pottery into that which is strong, beautiful, and useful. He does this not because he is lacking in compassion. It is because he loves us like the father who refuses to let his child run out into the busy street. Rather, he disciplines the child to help him or her understand that some things are forbidden for one's own benefit. At the time such discipline is not appreciated but afterward the child can see that it was necessary for his own protection and growth. In like manner God sometimes trains us in ways that are not pleasant and it is only later that we can see how the discipline made us stronger and more Christlike (Heb. 12:5–12).

Closely connected with this is a fourth reason for suffering—it enables us to be more caring. The person who has suffered is often more sympathetic and better able to help others who are in need. Paul mentioned this at the beginning of his second letter to the Corinthians (1:3–7). When we suffer, he wrote, we are better able to understand and comfort others who suffer. This is important for anyone who wants to experience the joy of caring.

What about God's Power and God's Goodness?

These reasons, helpful as they may be, nevertheless avoid the questions raised at the beginning of this chapter. If God is all knowing and all powerful why doesn't he do something to stop suffering? If God is so concerned about us why does he permit pain? Perhaps no one has dealt with these questions more clearly than the late C. S. Lewis. When God created us, Lewis pointed out, he gave us the freedom to choose and to act. Having been given that freedom, humans were free to choose evil and that is exactly what they did.

We can, perhaps, conceive of a world in which God corrected the results of this abuse of free will by His creatures at every moment: so that a wooden beam became soft as grass when it was used as a weapon, and the air refused to obey me if I attempted to set up in it the sound waves that carry lies or insults. But such a world would be one in which wrong actions were impossible, and in which, therefore, freedom of the will would be void. . . . That God can and does, on occasions, modify the behaviour of matter and produce what we call miracles, is part of the Christian faith; but the very conception of a common, and therefore, stable, world, demands that these occasions be extremely rare. . . . Try to exclude the possibility of suffering which the order of nature and the existence of free wills involve, and you will find that you have excluded life itself.[5]

Machines and robots never suffer but this is because they have no free will and are programmed to act in a certain way. God in his love did not make us robots. He created us as free persons who have the right to abuse our freedom. Of course, God either could remove our freedom and hence remove our suffering, or he could leave us free with all of the pain that such freedom involves. Clearly he has chosen the latter course.

But what about God's goodness? Can a God who is good let free human beings hurt one another? Lewis answers this by suggesting that God's definition of goodness may differ from ours. We would like a God who is more like a grandfather—a benevolent old man who sits back to let us enjoy ourselves so that a good time is had by all.

Suppose a man with a new puppy took that attitude toward his dog. If the animal could do anything it wanted it would end up being wild—dirty, smelly, untrained, distrustful, and of no pleasure to its owner. Instead, because the man loves and enjoys the dog, he watches it, house trains it, teaches it not to steal, and limits some of its "natural" tendencies. In so doing, the dog becomes more loyal and comfortable than it would have been otherwise, and the man has a pet which brings him great pleasure.

Obviously such an analogy should not be pushed too far.

We are not dogs; neither are we God's "pets." But just as a man permits his animal to suffer as part of its training, so the God of this universe, in his goodness, permits us to be molded into creatures who can love him more and who in turn become individuals in whom God is well pleased.

Jesus' View of Suffering

Psychiatrist John White has suggested that Jesus showed several attitudes toward suffering.[6] One of these has already been mentioned. He rejected any idea that suffering always comes as a result of sin in the sufferer's life.

Jesus also resisted the idea that suffering was something which we should avoid. He came to this earth to die for our sins and he willingly suffered far beyond what any human being has had to experience.

In spite of this, however, Jesus never taught that Christians should look for opportunities to suffer. He never gave any indication that we should beat ourselves or cause self-inflicted suffering on the assumption that this would build up merit points with God. When suffering comes we accept it and learn from it, but it is not our responsibility to seek suffering. Instead, he told his followers that when persecution comes in one town, they should flee to the next (Matt. 10:23). "Take up your cross" does not mean "go out and find some place to suffer." Instead it means "be prepared to suffer if suffering comes along."

Jesus also taught that Christians ought to expect suffering, and he warned us not to be surprised if we are called upon to suffer because of our faith. Peter wrote about this in his first epistle. "Do not be surprised at the fiery ordeal among you, which comes upon you for your testing, as though some strange thing were happening to you; but to the degree that you share the sufferings of Christ, keep on rejoicing. . . . If anyone suffers as a Christian, let him not feel ashamed, but in that name let him glorify God" (1 Peter 4:12, 13, 16). The early Christians did suffer because of their beliefs, just as people around the world are suffering today.

Corrie ten Boom was a woman who spent almost a year living in the indescribable misery of a Nazi concentration camp. Several of her relatives died in prison. Following her release she wrote her life story—a story which subsequently was made into a full-length motion picture.

During the filming of this movie Corrie suggested to a friend that the film might some day be used to prepare people for suffering which could come in the future. In our period of history, at least in the Western world, we are experiencing a great popular interest in Christianity. But the day may come, perhaps in our own lifetime and in our own society, when Christians will be called upon to suffer intensely because of their faith. Like the early believers, and like Corrie ten Boom in Holland, we must be ready.

Learning to Suffer

How do we get ready? How can we prepare for suffering? Perhaps one way is to honestly face the fact that in life, all of us suffer at least sometimes. When I was in graduate school, we used to talk about a common attitude which says, "It may happen to others; it won't happen to me." This is the attitude that causes us to think: "Hundreds may die in car accidents during some holiday weekend, but of course I won't be one of them," or "A lot of smokers have heart attacks but certainly this won't happen to me so I can go on smoking." Clearly this is avoidance. It is a mental attitude which lets us go through life blithely ignoring the fact that suffering does come to all of us. Since we don't think about it, pain hits harder when it does come into our lives.

We ignore suffering when we avoid people who suffer and when we don't try to care for them. When we reach out to others who are suffering we not only experience the joy of caring but we prepare ourselves for that inevitable time when pain and grief will come into our own lives.

What do we do when that pain arrives? People who have suffered intensively have helped us to answer that question. Joni Eareckson, for example, spent many months trying to learn what God was teaching her and pretending that if she only could learn that lesson, then probably she would be healed. Eventually she moved from a bitter questioning to a humble trust. She learned that there is nothing wrong with questioning. And she discovered that this can distract us from learning to trust God in the midst of our pain. This was a lesson which Job had learned centuries earlier. He tried to understand and couldn't, but this did not lead to bitterness against God. Instead Job trusted him, regardless of the circumstances.

The sufferer also has a responsibility to be faithful, worshiping God as best one can and reaching out (like Corrie and Betsie ten Boom did in prison) to minister to others in so far as this is possible. Then, when all else fails, we have to stand back and commit ourselves to God, not because of the answers he gives, but because we know who he is—one who is sovereign, loving, all-knowing, all-powerful, and concerned about his creatures.

We who stand aside and watch people suffer sometimes expect to find bitterness and self-pity. Instead, we often find a renewed dependence upon God and a spirit of praise which shines forth and ministers to those of us who are not experiencing painful situations. Such radiant sufferers have learned to trust, and minister, in the midst of their pain. They can teach us much about suffering and about the joy of caring.

Why Not Me?

Recently I was having lunch in a restaurant with a former student when another of my previous students walked in, assisted by an elder from his church. Almost blind, diabetic, and with malfunctioning kidneys, my friend reported that a forthcoming kidney transplant would be the only way in which he could go on living.

In the crowded restaurant I looked at these two young men, both of whom have graduated from seminary. Both are sensitive, capable counselors, and both are deeply committed to serving Jesus Christ. One is healthy, athletic, and filled with energy. The other is sickly and very much aware that death may be imminent. Why should this one student be called upon to suffer so intensely while the other does not suffer physically at all? Why is Joni Eareckson paralyzed while her sister is healthy? Why did Betsie ten Boom die in prison when Corrie did not? These are questions which we cannot answer decisively.

As I grow older I am increasingly grateful for my health, abilities, and spiritual gifts, but it must also be remembered that "from everyone who has been given much shall much be required" (Luke 12:48). We who are without constant pain have a special obligation to serve God diligently because we have been given special strength and physical stamina.

One of the ways in which we serve God most effectively is to care for those who have special needs—to give love, practical assistance, and hope to those who suffer. We don't prepare for suffering or experience the joy of caring by withdrawing and closing our eyes to the suffering in the world. Instead we reach out as Jesus did to show concern, compassion, and sensitivity to those who need someone to care.

5

The How of Caring

BELINDA WONG WAS born in Taiwan, became a Christian while she was studying at the University of Wisconsin, and decided, following graduation, to enroll for further studies in a theological seminary.

That was where I first met her. She was one of my students—intelligent, sensitive to people, and deeply committed to Jesus Christ. Belinda was the first woman ever to receive a Master of Divinity degree at Trinity Evangelical Divinity School, and she went on to join the staff of InterVarsity Christian Fellowship working especially among the Chinese students in the Chicago-Milwaukee area.

Prior to her conversion, Belinda's life had not been easy, and it must have come as a great shock one day to discover that she had cancer. The doctors operated and performed a mastectomy. Then they did another. She had cobalt treatments, drug therapy, and various operations, but the disease continued to creep steadily throughout her body.

One thing that concerned Belinda greatly was her mother back home in Taiwan. Belinda's mother was Buddhist, a poor widow, with only one child. When it became apparent that this daughter would never return home to Taiwan, the Chinese churches in North America took an offering and raised enough money to bring Belinda's mother to the United States. Before long, the old lady became a Christian and joined the hundreds of fellow believers who were praying for Belinda's healing.

But Belinda kept growing worse. The mother announced that, in accordance with her culture, she would commit suicide if her daughter died because there was no social security in Taiwan and there would be no one to look after an aging childless widow.

One night, a few weeks later, Belinda lost consciousness and quietly passed away, but by then her mother had developed a new perspective on life.

"I will go back to Taiwan," she said. "My daughter dedicated her life to telling other people about Jesus Christ and I will carry on Belinda's work at home—telling my neighbors that the God of Christianity is the true God."

This is a moving conclusion to a sad story, but it leaves us with a difficult question: why was there no healing for Belinda in spite of the prayers of hundreds of people? In contrast, why have other sufferers improved—some even in dramatic and seemingly miraculous ways?

These questions about healing raise some crucial issues for anyone who really wants to be involved in the joy of caring.

Some Assumptions about Healing

Several years ago I was invited to participate in a conference on healing. The meeting, which lasted for two days, was attended by doctors, pastors, lay people, and professional counselors. I was the last speaker on the program, and in listening to those who came before me, I began to formulate some assumptions about healing (and about caring).

First, healing is desirable. This is not as ridiculous a beginning as it may seem. By his words and actions Jesus clearly taught that sickness was undesirable and that healing was a good thing. As Morton Kelsey has noted, one could never imagine Jesus saying, "Enjoy your sickness. Go your way and make something of your pain. It is better for you than the mischief you might be getting into otherwise." The apostle Paul's thorn in the flesh helped him to grow spiritually and to control his pride, but

> Paul did not say that God sent it (the sickness) or that it was a good thing. He only made clear that God did not take it away because it gave Paul the weakness, humility, and poverty of spirit which he needed for God to be manifest in his life. I am sure that God would have preferred Paul minus his pride and his thorn. But even if it is assumed from this passage (2 Cor. 12:7–9) that God was responsible for the ailment, this did not keep Paul from healing other people and commending the healing ministry.[1]

Second, healing occurs in a variety of settings. It often takes place in hospitals, clinics, or doctors' offices, but healing also occurs in homes, churches, prayer meetings, and educational institutions. In addition, at least some genuine healing probably occurs in healing services and at Catholic shrines such as Lourdes in southern France— although, in their enthusiasm believers in such divine healings often appear to make exaggerated claims of success. Of 41 healings which are recorded in the Gospels, none took place in a clinic, only three or four occurred in a home, some happened in the temple, but most took place on the street. Caring and healing, therefore, are not limited to institutional settings, important as these may be. We must care for people where they are and recognize that a lot of caring and healing takes place in settings where we might least expect this to happen.

Third, healing occurs in a variety of ways. One does not need to be a physician or a nurse to recognize that the medical profession has literally thousands of techniques which can be used to heal broken bodies and bring people back to a state of health. Perhaps it is less widely recognized that professional counselors also have a great variety of techniques. Even within Christian circles there are different approaches to counseling, each of which seems to work with at least some people.[2]

There is no one "guaranteed-to-work" correct or biblical way to care for others. We each have unique personalities and individualized problems which are not like those of anyone else. In caring, therefore, we don't apply some universal magical formula to everyone. Instead, we show love, concern, and respect for individual differences, trusting that God will enable us to provide the unique care that each person needs.

Fourth, healing is at least partially a mystery. The issues of pain and suffering discussed in the previous chapter also apply to healing. We can try to understand how or why healing occurs, and we can attempt to comprehend why some people—like Belinda Wong—are not healed, but our understanding will always be incomplete. We do not completely know why some people respond to treatment and others do not, why some physicians and counselors are more effective than others, why and how some of our procedures work as they do and why others do not. We do not know the reasons for God's apparent intervention or lack of intervention in specific cases.

There is much about healing and caring that we do know, however. An understanding of these healing principles can help us to be more compassionate and better able to care for people in need.

Principles of Healing and Caring

How can we really care for another individual? There is evidence to suggest that caring is most effective when the following conditions are present.

There is a deep concern for people on the part of the one who cares. Perhaps no principle of caring has been better established by scientific research. Several years ago, for example, an attempt was made to discover what makes a good counselor. Those who proved to be successful succeeded not so much because of their level of training or ability to use complicated techniques. As we mentioned in chapter 2, the best people-helpers were those who demon-

THE JOY OF CARING / 61

strated three personal traits: understanding, warmth, and genuineness.[3]

When we're hurting it is a comfort to know that someone has understanding and tries to see problems from the point of view of the one who hurts. *Warmth* involves a friendly concern that might be expressed verbally but more often is seen in the caring person's mannerisms and acts of compassion. *Genuineness* means that the caring person is willing to share of himself or herself without any hint of phoniness or insincerity.

Stated in another way, caring is most likely to be effective when love and compassion are present. More than any other person who has ever lived, Jesus showed compassion (Luke 7:13; Matt. 4:23, 24). He came to earth in the first place because of divine love (John 3:16) and he expects that his followers will be characterized by the kind of love described in 1 Corinthians 13. Love has been described as the mark of a Christian. Clearly it is also the mark of the person who cares effectively.

There is hope and expectation. When a person in need has lost hope, it is encouraging to discover that there are still other people whose hope persists. This is especially true when a doctor of the patient's family expresses hope and expectation. In a recent study at Johns Hopkins University Medical School, researchers concluded that healing is stimulated when a patient has confidence in the healer and his or her methods, an optimistic outlook, and a hopeful mental state.[4] Sometimes the big difference between whether or not improvement occurs is the hope expressed by the one who cares. And even when all hope of recovery is gone, it still is encouraging to recognize that the God of the universe is sovereign and unwilling to permit anything that is not for our ultimate good. That, in itself, is a reason for hoping.

We must be careful, however, not to assume that healing always depends on how strongly we hope, how firmly we believe, or how persistently we pray. Consider the healings recorded in the Bible. The woman with the issue of blood was healed because she had faith (Matt. 9:20–22). The nobleman's son was healed because of the faith of someone (his father) other than the one who was sick (John 4:46–54). In Gethsemane the servant's ear was restored but apparently no one had faith except Jesus, who was the healer (Luke 22:47–53). In contrast, Paul had great faith in God's ability to heal and prayed about this on several occasions, but healing didn't come (2 Cor. 12:7–10). Then there was the time when there was no faith and not much (if any) healing either (Matt. 13:58). Sometimes, then, people pray, healing comes and problems are resolved. At other times it appears that our requests for healing are not granted. It is difficult, therefore, and probably impossible, for us to know when our prayers will be answered as we hope and when; instead, God will show that he has a better plan.

The caring person has some helping skills. With all of this emphasis on love and hope it would be easy to conclude that the skill of a physician or counselor is of no importance. I have never had surgery, but if this ever becomes necessary I surely will seek a doctor who has surgical skills rather than hiring someone who is known around the hospital as one who is "loving and hopeful but incompetent." Paul Tournier, the well-known Swiss physician and counselor, has spent most of his adult life urging doctors to develop a personal interest in their patients, but Tournier stresses again and again that the physician should also be as skilled and professionally capable as possible. In all of healing there surely is a place for professional competence.

The same is true in counseling. If we are to be effective in caring for people, we must learn to be perceptive, insightful, able to listen carefully, skillful in asking questions, and capable practitioners of our counseling techniques. The Bible gives no justification for hiding sloppy craftsmanship behind spiritual piety. We need workmen who have no reason to be ashamed of their technical performance as healers and carers.

But what about the nonprofessional? What about the person who wants to help but has had no formal training in counseling and caring? Currently there are a number of books available which describe counseling skills and which teach people how to be more effective in caring for one another.[5] In addition, lay training seminars are being held with increasing frequency in different parts of the world. But even without this training we can help one another if we sincerely try to listen and understand while, at the same time, we encourage people to see a pastor or a professional counselor when we are no longer able to help.

There is an attempt to reduce stress. It is well known that internal conflict, tension, anxiety, anger, interpersonal dissension, fear, guilt, grief, disappointment, failure, and a host of other stresses can all lead to physical and psychological breakdown.[6] In a very real sense the love, hope, and skills which we have discussed above are all geared toward reducing stress, but for healing to occur, we must directly help people uncover, understand, and (in practical ways) deal with the basic causes of their problems. Sometimes we need to help people find meaning in life, deal with underlying sin, talk through anxious situations, or learn how to get along with others.[7]

The Bible was not written as a psychiatric textbook, but the Word of God does give some principles for good interpersonal relationships, some techniques for changing behavior, some ways of dealing with sin, and some practical guidelines for dealing with stress. Jesus came to help people live an abundant life on earth and to prepare for eternal life in heaven (John 10:10; 3:16). There can be no higher calling than to follow in his steps by helping people cope more effectively with the cares of this life and prepare for the next.

There is freedom from personal hangups in the carer. As you undoubtedly have heard, there is a popular idea that people who go into professional counseling do so because they have not been able to solve their own problems. It surely *is* true that some professionals enter the field of counseling because they are searching for ways to straighten out their own lives and marriages. In addition, since professional counseling can be very draining and difficult it is probable that some people who enter the field cannot handle the pressures that come from their work. A caring person who is bogged down with personal worries, illnesses, or pressures from work can be distracted by these problems and thus become less effective in caring for others. The mature carer is willing to face his or her personal stresses, to do something about them, and to accept caring, love, and encouragement from others.

There is an acknowledgment of the lordship of Jesus Christ. The Scriptures repeatedly declare that God is sovereign in the universe whether or not this fact is realized and acknowledged by humans. God through Christ created the world (Col. 1:16, 17), and it is by divine power that he holds everything together (Heb. 1:1–3). If sickness or problems come, it is only because these are permitted by God. This is one of the messages that we learn clearly from the Book of Job.

I do not believe that it is only Christians who can care for people effectively. We all know that nonbelieving physicians, counselors, and others can and do bring about improvement in the lives of their patients. God works through these healers and uses them even when they ignore or deny the Lordship of Christ.

Wouldn't it be better, however, if helpers put themselves willingly in the service of the One who ultimately permits and frequently brings about healing? In a book for pastoral counselors I once suggested that spiritual maturity could have a bearing on one's effectiveness in caring for and helping others. The effective helper:

> first must be a Christian, by having personally experienced new birth by believing that the risen Christ is the Son of God. Then, as in the day of Moses . . . counselors should be capable, God-fearing, honest, readily available and willing to get help when they encounter difficult cases (Exodus 18:21–22). The counselor should also be a student who is thoroughly familiar with the word of God (II Tim. 2:15) and a man or woman who seeks to be a follower of Christ whose very name is wonderful counselor.[8]

The Art of Caring

In the preceding pages we have made several references to an Old Testament figure named Job. According to the Bible, Job was a morally upright, religious man who had a fine family, social status, great wealth, and apparently good health. Then, one day, everything fell apart. Job did not know that God and the devil had been discussing him in heaven. The only thing Job knew was that he had lost his health and all of his possessions, and that his family members were all dead except for a wife whose critical attitude apparently was creating marital tension. It is little wonder that Job was angry, discouraged, and seemingly overwhelmed by the pressures of his life.

Shortly after all of these calamities, three of Job's friends came to sympathize and bring comfort. For several days they just sat with him, but then they began to talk. They criticized Job and argued that the problems must have come because of sin in his life. They seemed to be uncomfortable with Job's anger and could not accept the fact that a loving God would have permitted such tragedy for any reason other than a punishment for sin.

Here were three people who came to care but who criticized instead. They came to comfort but instead they condemned and brought no real help to Job when he needed help so desperately.

Then, along came a man named Elihu. He was younger than the others and apparently had been waiting for his elders to finish before he began to speak. Elihu was a man who cared and as a result he really helped Job. There were several things about Elihu's caring that made a difference.

First, Elihu listened. Unlike the other comforters who had spent their time talking and giving advice, Elihu apparently had been quiet, trying to understand (Job 32:11, 12). As a result of this listening, he knew what concerned Job, and he was able, as a result, to really meet Job's needs.

Listening is the most important step in learning how to care, but listening isn't easy. Most of us have a great tendency to talk and give advice, sometimes before we have even heard the other person's problem. Listening lets needy persons express themselves, ventilate some of their feelings, and get a better perspective on their problems. All this gives the carer a clearer understanding of the other person's needs and a greater ability to help.

Second, Elihu was involved. He was not a passive observer who watched Job suffer without feeling some of the pain. Elihu sensed Job's struggle. He sought to be impartial and pointed out that he, like Job, was a human being who came alongside not to condemn or to take a superior attitude, but to care (Job 32:21; 33:6, 7).

Third, Elihu engaged in dialogue. Paul Tournier, who was mentioned earlier in this chapter, reports that he helps people best when he can dialogue with them. He encourages people to share while he tries to understand and to think of ways in which he can be helpful. Elihu had somewhat of the same attitude. He had some things to say to Job but he invited Job to respond and they talked over their ideas together (Job 33:32, 33).

None of us likes to be on the receiving end of a lecture; neither do we like to have someone give us advice without providing opportunity for us to respond. Real caring means that we respect each other so much that we can share, encourage, support, and talk together.

Fourth, Elihu confronted. Have you ever noticed that problems sometimes come because of inefficiency, foolish actions, or sinful behavior? Sometimes then, we can help people best by caring enough to confront others with their own harmful attitudes and actions.[9]

Confrontation is not the same as telling people what to do. According to William Hulme, telling is the most often used method of communication but it is also the least effective.

Telling is ineffective because it implies *telling off*. It has within it the barb of an attack which moves the hearer to erect his defenses. By presuming to know better, the teller places the hearer in a subordinate position. . . . Confrontation is less impulsive and more efficient than telling. . . . When the counselor confronts the counselee, he cares enough to risk offending him in order to help him. . . .

Confronting means presenting something to the counselee that he seemingly needs help in perceiving. It may be an insight into himself or his relationships that is slow in coming. It may be an alternative decision that the counselee seemingly has resistance to considering. It may be a suggestion that carries with it a touch of a shock because of the counselee's indisposition to hear it. It may be a challenge to act because the counselor senses the counselee is taking recourse in inaction. . . . The very fact that confronting may be necessary is an indication that it is not easy to do.[10]

Elihu confronted Job with some of his faulty attitudes, and as a result Job was able to make some changes.

Finally, Elihu pointed to God. Undoubtedly one of the things that helped Job the most was that Elihu didn't try to defend God, to make excuses for God's actions, or push the blame onto Job. After the confrontation Elihu simply pointed Job's eyes to God. "Behold, God is mighty but does not despise any; He is mighty in strength of understanding." Then Elihu spoke of God's dealings with men (Job 36:5 and following), and before long, God himself began to speak. Job soon saw that although there were things which he could not understand, he nevertheless could place his trust in God. This put things in a new perspective, and Job improved. He had met a man who applied the principles of healing and who demonstrated that he had learned the art of caring.

Part II
The Priorities of Caring

6

Caring about Ourselves

IT HAD BEEN a busy day and when we reached the motel room shortly before midnight I threw my coat on the bed, sank into a chair, and kicked off my shoes. My associate, with whom I conducted seminars, stretched out on the other bed and as so often happened we began to talk.

"Gary," he asked, "what was wrong with you tonight? Your talk wasn't all that good, and you seemed to be very concerned about whether or not the people liked what you were saying."

I didn't like to admit it, but I knew he was right. In the evening seminar I had been less concerned about having a ministry than about being appreciated by the people in the audience. But the harder I tried to do a good job, the worse my speaking seemed to become. From my perspective the whole evening had been a disaster, and as we talked I began to think that my work was poor, that I probably wasn't any good as a speaker. Before long, as so often happens to all of us, I began to feel sorry for myself, and this self-pity led to discouragement.

As we talked further, however, I began to get a new perspective on myself and on my ministry. It was a perspective that was to change my whole way of thinking and liberate me from a frustrating life style of trying to prove my worth to others and to myself.

Many of us, I suspect, have spent a lot of time trying to build an image, or to construct a way of living designed to impress others and win their acceptance. For example, we may want to be known as a successful businessman, a good parent, an ideal Christian, someone with a superb family, or a problem-free individual who "has it all together." We try to live up to our image, but usually this is impossible. As a result, we end up in frustration, afraid that people will see behind our masks and discover what we are really like.

Have you ever considered how people try to deal with their feelings of inferiority? Some of us respond with a façade of self-confidence and social finesse. We seem so capable and self-assured that others are impressed, and occasionally we even are able to convince ourselves that we no longer feel inferior.

Others like to boast about their inadequacies and almost take pride in having an "inferiority complex." Sometimes we talk about our inadequacies in an unconscious attempt to manipulate others into saying that "really we aren't as bad as we say." This gives us a temporary sense of well-being.

Then there are those who deal with their insecurities by associating with the famous and the successful. This leads to a self-deceptive game which says, "Since I know all of these important people, I must be important too."

Several years ago, Paul Tournier wrote a whole book about this problem of our own insecurities:

> We are all in the habit of classifying people into two categories, the strong and the weak. There are those who seem doomed to be defeated and trampled upon. They have been so often beaten in this universal free-for-all that they are always expecting it to happen again, and this saps their strength. Those who know them also expect it, and gather strength and assurance for themselves from the fact. . . . On the other hand, the same intuition warns him of the strength of the strong, so that he adapts towards them an attitude of timidity or deference which confirms their strength. . . .
>
> The truth is that human beings are much more alike than they think. What is difficult is the external mask, sparkling

or disagreeable, their outward reaction, strong or weak. These appearances, however, hide an identical inner personality. The external mask, the outward reaction, deceives everybody, the strong as well as the weak. All men, in fact, are weak. All are weak because they all are afraid. They are all afraid of being trampled underfoot. They are all afraid of their inner weakness being discovered. They all have secret faults; they all have a bad conscience on account of certain acts which they would like to keep covered up. They are all afraid of other men and of God, of themselves, of life and of death. . . . What distinguishes men from each other is not their inner nature, but the way in which they react to this common distress.[1]

Caring and Ourselves

Have you ever read a novel in which some one of the characters is described? Perhaps you've read about the person's appearance, traits, mannerisms, abilities, personal quirks, strong points, or weaknesses.

Now let's suppose for a minute that the author was describing you. What do you think might be said? Then go one step further and assume you were describing yourself. What would you say about your appearance, your abilities and mannerisms, your personality, your strong points, and your weaknesses?

Perhaps most of us would answer that there is much about ourselves which we don't like. We may not like our appearance, for example. We may feel inferior to others in intelligence, social charm, vocational success, or spiritual commitment. These self-critical attitudes are so common that according to one estimate perhaps 95 percent of the people in our society have at least mild feelings of inferiority.

When human beings were first created, God made us in his image but before long our ancestors fell into sin. Death and suffering entered the world, our relationship with God was severed, and the human race found itself in need of a Savior. That Savior, Jesus Christ, came to earth in human form, died on the cross to pay for our sins, rose victorious over death, and went back into heaven where he now brings our prayer requests before God the Father.

In helping ourselves, therefore, it is important to remember repeatedly what God thinks about us. He made us, loves us, sent his Son to die for us, makes us into new people if we invite him into our lives (2 Cor. 5:17), gives each of us special gifts and responsibilities while we are here on earth (1 Cor. 12:4–6; 12:11), and promises us eternal life in heaven. It's true, of course, that everyone sins—even Christians—but he forgives every time we fall and then confess our sin (1 John 1:8–10). In God's eyes believers are special people, loved, forgiven, cleansed, and assured of a painless and glorious future with God after death.

In the meantime, God accepts us as we are now. Because of Christ's payment for our sins, we can be forgiven and we don't have to do anything to gain this approval.

I have known this intellectually for many years, but it was during that motel room discussion that I began to recognize its practicality for my own life. I began to realize that as a Christian my task is to follow Jesus Christ to the best of my ability—but I don't have to perform. I don't have to write another book or give a good seminar talk to be accepted and approved by God. All he wants from me is commitment of my life to him. He has even sent his Holy Spirit to live within me and to help me when I'm inclined not to obey or when I get distracted with my own push for success. That is a liberating realization! God's acceptance is not conditional. If we are Christians, we are already children of the King.

There is nothing wrong with recognizing our good points, accepting these as coming from God, and developing them. In contrast we should remember that there is nothing spiritual about condemning ourselves all the time, dwelling on our weaknesses, or boasting to ourselves and others about how incompetent we are. How we think of ourselves determines in large measure how we act and how we feel. When we see ourselves from God's perspective (as sinners who have been forgiven, made new, and completely accepted by the God of the universe), then our self-image should become more positive.

For many of us, however, the problem is not so much where we stand with God but where we stand with others. We feel inferior because we have learned to compare ourselves with people who are more skilled or successful than we are. The picture we have of ourselves often comes because we have failed or been belittled in the past. Sometimes we have sinned and feel guilt, self-condemnation, or inferiority as a result. We sometimes blindly ignore our feelings of inferiority while at other times we emphasize them by saying to ourselves, "I'm inferior and can't do anything." As a result we refuse to try anything new, or to risk failure.

Many of us deal with our inferiorities in two ways: the first assumes that we will always lose, and the second that we will always be striving. Let's consider the "always lose" situation first. Most of us have heroes—people in our own line of work who seem to do the job better than we can. The teacher will see other teachers who communicate better and seem to have better rapport with students. The housewife or mother looks at other homemakers who seem to be better organized and more efficient in handling their children. Most of the time we compare ourselves with someone who looks better and as a result we come out looking bad. As we improve in our work, our choice of models changes so we are always on the bottom.

In our desire to succeed, however, we also can put ourselves in an "always striving" situation. We believe that if we do something better we will look better and as a result others will be more accepting. But as our performance improves there is always someone to criticize us. We never feel really accepted because we can never perform in a way completely satisfying to everyone.

It is hardly surprising that in the midst of this kind of struggle, many people just give up. They assume that there is no way to succeed in this life so they do little to improve themselves or to mature psychologically, vocationally, or spiritually. When failure comes, they blame it on the fact that they are "no good anyway" and this becomes an excuse for not having tried.

In my motel room discussion, the liberating idea was the realization that since God loves me and since my worth depends solely on him, then it is not necessary for me to impress an audience, to "have it all together psychologically," to be a perfect Christian, or to be the leader in my vocation. In fact, I can rest secure in the fact that God loves me, that one or two close people love me, and that I am accepted by God and by these close friends even if I never succeed in anything for the rest of my life. My worth as an individual does not depend on my status, wealth, success, or reputation. God loves me and that is crucial. But there are also some people who love me just because I'm me, and that's important too.

What does this say about caring for ourselves? First, it is important to have others who accept and love us. The way to get such love and acceptance is not to manipulate people, trying to persuade them of the things about ourselves that even we don't truly believe. The way to get love and acceptance is to sincerely love and accept others. When we reach out to love and accept other people (with God's help), people love and accept us in return—not because of what we do, but because of who we are. Once again, therefore, we see that caring for others is the best way to care for ourselves.

Then, we need to stop comparing ourselves constantly with other people. Such comparisons often lead to despair (because we appear to be so much less capable than another) or to pride (because we seem to be so much better). Instead, it is more helpful to compare ourselves today with how we were last year at this time and then to keep on working, with God's help, to improve on our record so that we will be more capable and effective in the future. Perhaps at times we will need the help of a friend who can help us to see ourselves and our progress better than we might be able to see it alone.

In many respects this is a radical suggestion. From childhood we have learned to compare ourselves with others and to base our self-worth on our status, reputation, or position. We have overlooked the words of Jesus who said that our lives do not consist in how much we possess (Luke 12:15). Instead our worth is based first on our relationship with Jesus Christ and second on the support and acceptance that we have from those people in the body of Christ who love us because of who we are and not because of what we do.

Reaching to Maturity

None of this should be taken as an excuse for laziness or for satisfaction with the status quo. We need to be continually growing, learning, and moving toward greater maturity.

The extent to which one is mature has little to do with one's age in years. According to one psychologist[2] a mature individual shows at least five characteristics.

A realistic view of oneself and others. A maturing person asks, "What are the things that I do best?" "What are my strengths and weaknesses?" "What do other people think I do well?" "How do others see my strong and weak points?"

It is important to know one's strengths and weaknesses and to not overestimate or underestimate either. With a Christian there is, in addition, a sincere desire to see oneself and others as God sees us:[3] created in the divine image, fallen and in need of a Savior, redeemed and made into new creatures (if we have by an act of will confessed our sins and acknowledged the Lordship of Jesus Christ), endowed with spiritual gifts, and placed within the body of believers. A mature believer does not seek to be a superstar Christian, lording it over others or longing for popular acclaim. Maturity in Christ involves humility and recognizes that the essence of Christian living is found in the words of Jesus, "Whoever wishes to become great among you shall be your servant, and whoever wishes to be first among you shall be your slave" (Matt. 20:26, 27).

Acceptance of oneself and others. Acceptance is not the same as approval. Each of us might honestly accept the fact that he or she has certain fears, desires, insecurities, or temptations to sin, even though one might not approve of such things in his or her life. To honestly accept what we are, how we look, and the abilities that have been given by God can all be important steps in growing—sometimes beyond and sometimes in spite of our inner frustrations.

Immature people refuse to acknowledge their insecurities, failures, and disappointments. Often they are characterized by a harmful attitude of bitterness or unrealistic pride, and they show a tendency to be intolerant of weakness in others. The mature person, with God's help, can see beyond these imperfections, recognizing value and potential in others, especially in those brothers and sisters who are in the body of Christ.

An ability to live in the present but to have long-range goals. This is not as simple as it might at first seem. Many people live in the past, dwelling on previous successes or memories; others live in the future, dreaming of what life could be like. The mature person faces and makes the best of the present, but also shows a desire to plan realistically for the future, to form goals, and to move toward attaining these goals. Paul expressed both the ability to live in the present and a clear goal for the future when he wrote:

> I have learned to be content in whatever circumstances I am. I know how to get along with humble means, and I also know how to live in prosperity; in any and every circumstance I have learned the secret of being filled and going hungry, both of having abundance and suffering need. I can do all things through Him who strengthens me. . . .

> One thing I do: forgetting what lies behind and reaching forward to what lies ahead. I press on toward the goal for the prize of the upward call of God in Christ Jesus (Phil. 4:11–13; 3:13, 14).

A set of values—standards of right and wrong, good and bad. The mature person consciously chooses his or her own value system and makes it an integral part of life. The values of a mature Christian are based on the Bible—God's Word and God's standard for his created human beings. Mature Christians, to quote Elton Trueblood, are "willing to bet their life that Christ is right."[4] This gives us a stable guide to life and a purpose for living.

Immature people, however, have no clear standards. They vacillate in their thinking about what is right or wrong and they fail to make firm decisions about their values.

The developing of one's abilities and interests while still coping with the problems of everyday life. Mature people have interests, projects in which they are involved, concerns about others, a desire to obtain their fullest potential, and an ability to cope with the demands of daily living.

In contrast, immature people try to protect themselves from the pressures of life, from others and from things that are new and challenging. The mature Christian realizes that he or she has gifts from God to be developed and used to build up the church. This becomes one of the prime purposes for living.

If we are going to care for people and to help others care, it is important that we recognize individual differences in maturity. And it is also important to determine, with God's help and the help of one another, that we will move toward maturity in our own lives.

Winning over Weariness

This is a tall order. It isn't easy to be maturing all the time, to be reaching out to others, to be sensitive enough to care in the face of human needs. If we have any real desire to care for people, most of us discover that we get tired periodically and need rest if we are to care effectively.

The Bible instructs us to "not lose heart in doing good, for in due time we shall reap if we do not grow weary" (Gal. 6:9). Surely the apostle Paul, who wrote these words, must have known about the weariness that so often comes when we are involved in helping others. Involved with so many hurting individuals, caring people sometimes "burn out"—like a fire that glows in splendor for a time and then fades into ashes which give little heat and even less light.

How can we be caring, compassionate, effective helpers without burning out? There are several answers.

First, we need spiritual strength. Fire goes out when it runs out of fuel and oxygen. According to Ephesians 6, believers are in a battle with spiritual forces of darkness and wickedness. Satan is intent on weakening and if possible extinguishing our caring activities. We cannot fight this battle alone. Regular periods of meditation and Bible study are absolutely essential if we are to be effective as caring servants of Jesus Christ. In addition, it is extremely important that we consistently spend time in prayer asking God to give us the right perspective on our work and on how we should spend our time.

Ross Foley, a Minnesota pastor, wrote about this recently in his book on weariness.

> The Gospels convince the reader that Jesus was tender, loving and compassionately responsive to the pains, hurts and cries of people around Him. But Jesus was never captured by His compassion, never enslaved by the spontaneous, never tyrannized by the urgent, and never victimized by the incessant interruptions that inundated Him. . . . He refused to respond to the thing of urgent importance when that response would hinder Him from pursuing the thing of ultimate importance. . . . How did Jesus know that the time had come to ignore the urgent and pursue the ultimate?
>
> Jesus had an active prayer life. . . . Prayer is the key to living a pressure-packed life without growing weary in well-doing. Why? Because in prayer God shows us the difference between the urgent and the ultimate. He delivers us from perpetual motion and, instead, enables us to have a peaceful, productive life, faithful to Him and free from frenzy. And to be free from frenzy is to be free from fatigue.[5]

Second, we need to recognize our limitations. Many people tend to push themselves almost beyond the limits of humanity. It is important to remember that Jesus never expected one person to change the whole world or to do all the caring. Some people do not seem to realize this. Some of us try to convince ourselves that we have more ability or more energy than God has given us. Often this attitude comes, once again, because we compare ourselves with people who seem to accomplish more and get along with less rest than we can.

Perhaps each of us needs to recognize that there are limitations beyond which we cannot go without breaking down emotionally or collapsing physically. Here again, another person can often help us to know just how far we can push ourselves.

This brings us to a *third suggestion: we need body support.* There is no such thing as do-it-yourself Christianity or make-it-on-your-own spiritual maturity. Christianity is a way of life built around the person of Jesus Christ and characterized by love for one another. We need people to pray for us and with us. We need friends and colleagues who accept us, encourage us, and care for us; people whom we can encourage and care for in return. Each of us needs at least one or two people with whom we can pray, be open and honest in confessing our faults, and be free of any pressure to succeed or to perform. We each need someone with whom we can cry, knowing that at such times we will be accepted, understood, and assured that our personal hurts will be kept confidential.

How can we find such a person or persons? Look around. Undoubtedly there are others, perhaps in your own family or your own church who, like you, long for such caring support. It is not too simple to conclude that a powerful God who answers prayer can also lead you to others who can give and receive the support which prevents burnout.

Fourth, we need time alone. Going away for times of rejuvenation often is more a fantasy wish than a practical reality. Many of us, I suspect, never seem to relax and sometimes we feel guilty about taking time off—even though God himself has commanded us to rest. He gave us an example when he rested after creating the world. Jesus, too, took time away from the crowds to meditate, to pray, to rest, and to spend time in relaxation.

It is not true that the harder we work, the more we accomplish. After a while we discover that in spite of long hours and driving activities, our efficiency decreases. We cannot be effective in caring for people without taking regular breaks for physical, mental, social, and spiritual rejuvenation—even if these breaks put us out of contact temporarily with some of the very people who need help.

Such breaks give us a new perspective on caring. They help us to clear our minds of attitudes which can overwhelm us when we are involved intensively with other people. By pulling away we get a better perspective on how we are spending our time, on the people whom we want to help, and on our priorities. Such a perspective enables us to return to our work with enthusiasm and helps us to overcome some of the weariness of caring.

Finally, we need to share responsibilities. The easy way to get a job done is to do it ourselves. This principle probably guides many of our actions, but isn't it interesting to note that God didn't work this way. He used imperfect men and women to accomplish his purposes. Jesus surely didn't need the disciples. He could have accomplished the evangelism of the world in another way. Nevertheless he trained the disciples, gave them responsibilities, and risked not having the job done perfectly so they could learn and share in serving God.

There have been times in our marriage when my work has piled up or when something is bothering me which I have not discussed with my wife. I've discovered that it is difficult for her to know that I am pressured or distressed and not know what is really bothering me. She would rather know the details of what's going on than to have to guess what might be concerning me. When I share with her, I find that this is therapeutic for me and very often helpful for her. She is able to pray for me more diligently, can make suggestions to help, and often can take some action which will help relieve the pressure on me.

Any good relationship must be built on truth even when the truth hurts. My task as a caring person is not to rid myself of guilt feelings at someone else's expense or to use other people to do the things I should be doing myself. I must remember that Christians are part of a supportive caring body. We exist to help one another and at times it is important to tell someone what he or she can do to care for us. Such sharing is an effective way both to help others and to care for ourselves.

7

Caring about Others

WHEN YOU HEAR the word "religion," what comes into your mind? Think about that for a minute.

Perhaps you think of churches and steeples, choirs and song books, clergy and sermons. Maybe religion reminds you of worshipful experiences and of closeness with other churchgoers. Perhaps the term implies phoniness, irrelevance, and even hypocrisy.

The Bible, which might be expected to define the word, almost never mentions religion except for one notable exception. In the Book of James we are given three characteristics of religion, none of which has anything to do with outward acts of worship.

The truly religious person is described first as one who can control his or her tongue. What we say, especially in times of stress, is a good measure of where we are spiritually. Before we lash out verbally or begin to criticize we should ask ourselves: Is what I want to say true? Is it kind? Will it do any good for this to be said? If our speech could be guided by these three questions, we would not only be more religious; we would be more caring. Such verbal self-control comes slowly, however, and undoubtedly it is something which we learn through practice. It comes as we let the Holy Spirit be more consistently in control of both our lives and our tongues—especially when we are angry or frustrated.

A second mark of true religion, according to the Bible, is that the religious person visits "orphans and widows in their distress" (James 1:27). In the ancient world these people could not fend for themselves. Often they were exploited or poorly treated and there was no social security to take care of their needs. To visit such persons, showing a loving interest and personal concern, was not something which usually brought forth praise from those who stood aside and watched. But in the sight of God, such compassion is the mark of true religion—far more important than pious actions or a holier-than-thou religiosity (Mic. 6:6–8; Hos. 6:6; Matt. 9:13, 12:7). Jesus even taught that whenever we help someone in need—the hungry, the thirsty, the stranger, the person who is poor or sick or in prison—we are doing these acts for Christ himself (Matt. 25:35–40, 45). Such compassionate caring actions for all people who are in distress, including orphans and widows, are at the core of true religion.

A third mark of religion is that we should keep ourselves "unstained by the world." We live in a society which is characterized by rebellion against God and a general disinterest in biblical teachings. The truly religious person, however, does not conform to the standards and values of modern society. Instead, he or she is transformed into a person who seeks to live in accordance with the will of God. Such an individual has a mind which is surrendered to God and which thinks thoughts that are pure, kind, and gracious rather than thoughts which are critical, negative, and destructive (Rom. 12:1, 2; Phil. 4:8).

True religion and true caring clearly go together. To control our tongues, to reach out to those who are in distress, and (so far as is possible) to keep from becoming squeezed into the philosophy of our age—all of this is at the basis of caring for others.

But have you noticed that others do not always appreciate our attempts to care? Some people criticize when we try to help. Some turn away. Others are difficult to help because, quite frankly, they are people whom we do not like or individuals with whom we have difficulty in getting along.

When we have trouble with interpersonal relations, it is not easy to care.

Perhaps all of us, at least periodically, have conflicts and difficulties in getting along with others. Numerous articles and books have been written about this, most of which discuss understanding, communication, kindness, and the things we can do to live in peace with one another.[1] Many of these suggestions are helpful but often they rely solely on human potential and the ability of people to get along in their own strength. To get along better with others, and hence to care more effectively, we first must look to God, seeking his guidance and wisdom in building better human relationships. Then we can look at ourselves, look at others, and work on the principles of better communication. In this chapter we will discuss each of these in more detail.

Looking to God

It is easy to overlook the fact that people cannot live in real harmony with each other and truly care for one another until they are first in harmony with God. Writing in Germany on the eve of the Second World War, Dietrich Bonhoeffer observed that:

> Among men there is strife. . . . Without Christ there is discord between God and man and between man and man. Christ became the Mediator and made peace with God and among men. Without Christ we should not know God, we could not call upon Him, nor come to Him. But without Christ we also would not know our brother, nor could we come to him. The way is blocked by our own ego. Christ opened up the way to God and to our brother. Now Christians can live with one another in peace; they can love and serve one another; they can become one. But they can continue to do so only by way of Jesus Christ. Only in Jesus Christ are we one, only through Him are we bound together.[2]

This is the kind of statement that we need to read slowly and more than once. It is also a statement with which we might disagree. We all know of nonbelievers who seem to get along pretty well with each other. And don't we know of people who claim to be Christians but are divided by conflict, jealousy, complaining, and even anger?

According to the Bible (1 Cor. 2:14, 3:3) people can be categorized into three groups: natural, immature, and spiritual. The natural person is the nonbeliever who, through ignorance or deliberate rejection, has never invited Christ to control his or her life. Such individuals control their own lives. Although many reach a high ethical plane and show admirable qualities, they nevertheless are all sinners in need of a Savior. They follow their personal inclinations, and, as a result, there is complaining, jealousy, and, at times, even fighting in an attempt to get what they want. Often such people really care for others but their very nature leads to tension and strife.

Unlike the natural person, immature Christians have recognized their sinful separation from God, have confessed their sins and invited Christ into their lives, and clearly are believers. But such people do not have a satisfying Christian life because they are spiritually immature. Their lives are characterized by struggles, frustration, and often failure. They believe in Christ but are unwilling to let him guide their lives. As a result, these people show many characteristics of the nonbeliever including envy, strife, and a difficulty in getting along with others (1 Cor. 3:3). This, of course, can hinder their ability to care.

In contrast to all this are those spiritual Christians who have accepted Christ as Lord and Savior and who seek on a daily basis to bring their lives under divine control. These people are maturing spiritually, and their lives can be characterized by a growing love, peace, patience, and gentleness, all of which come from God and increase one's ability to get along with others (Gal. 5:22, 23).

If we really want to care for people, we must learn to get along with them. If we want to get along we begin by looking to God, submitting ourselves to him, and asking him to make us more Christlike. Then we can trust that he will give us a love which is patient and kind, not jealous or arrogant—a love which helps us to relate to others and then to care more effectively for one another.

Looking Within

When people are controlled by the Spirit of God, do they automatically get along with each other? Does efficient caring arise spontaneously in the life of the committed believer? For some people, the answers to these questions would be "yes," but for most of us relating to others and caring for them is something we learn.

When people are not getting along well, have you ever noticed how often they try to blame someone else for the problem? Children and their parents often blame each other for disagreements and misunderstandings. Labor and management, students and professors, members of different political parties, factions in the church, and even husbands and wives at times accuse each other of causing difficulties which may arise between them. In his Sermon on the Mount Jesus commented on this tendency. "Don't criticize," he stated. "Why do you look at the speck of sawdust in your brother's eye and pay no attention to the plank in your own eye?" He called such thinking hypocritical and instructed us to first "Take the plank out of your own eye, and then you will see clearly to remove the speck from your brother's eye" (Matt. 7:3–5, NIV). On another occasion, when Jesus was asked to intervene in a dispute over some property, he told the man bringing the complaint to begin by checking his own attitudes and values (Luke 12:13–15).

In one of his books, psychologist John Drakeford described a hypothetical interview with a lady who had come complaining about her marriage problems and about the terrible actions of her husband. The woman wanted the counselor to "straighten out" the husband. Instead the counselor explained that since marriage is a shared experience—"when something snarls it up, it is never a matter of one person being wrong and the other person being right."

After admitting that the husband probably was acting

badly, the counselor said to the wife: "Let us suppose your husband is 90 percent wrong. Would you be willing to accept 10 percent of the blame for the difficulties you presently face?" To discuss the husband's shortcomings in his absence might have pleased the wife, but it would do nothing to change him. Instead the counselor persuaded the wife to acknowledge and start working on her own weaknesses—even though these may only have been a small part of the problem.[3]

Surely, when we aren't getting along with someone else, we ought first to look inward to see if we are the ones whose attitudes and viewpoints are creating at least part of the tension.

It is easier, of course, to put the blame on someone else when problems arise. None of us likes to admit failure or to acknowledge that the fault may be our own. This can be threatening, and if I am at fault, even partially, it follows that I must change. That can be inconvenient and difficult.

When other people are hard to get along with or when they are having difficulties, our responsibility is not to sit back, criticize, and find excuses for doing nothing. We need to ask:

Am I part of the problem?

Is there some way in which I can change to make things better?

Even if the other person has brought on his or her own problems, is there something I can do to help?

Looking at our own attitudes or values, and pondering the reasons for our own lack of involvement (or unwillingness to change) can all be helpful steps toward becoming more caring.

Looking to Others

It is only after looking at our relationship with God and considering our own actions or attitudes that we are in a position to evaluate the attitudes and needs of others. Of course, other people often are at fault. They do criticize, gossip, bring on their own problems, refuse to cooperate, and sometimes ignore us or push us away whenever we try to help, apologize, or make restitution.

At such times, we first must try to understand. Do you remember the old Indian motto which says that you can't understand another man until you have walked a mile in his moccasins? It is difficult to understand another person until you have tried to see things from his or her perspective.

Several years ago one of my daughters convinced me that we should see a movie entitled *Freaky Friday*. It was the story of a teenage girl and her mother who through some magical fantasy were able to exchange bodies for a day. The mother saw the whole world through the eyes of a teenager; the teenager saw everything from the point of view of the mother. The resulting confusion was hilarious, and in the end, when the mother and daughter returned to normal, they had a far greater understanding of each other's life style and difficulties in trying to get along.

When we try to see things from another person's point of view it does not necessarily follow that we will accept or agree with that point of view. Neither is it likely that we will completely understand. Nevertheless, we can try to see things "as if" we were the other person, even though we never can get into that other person's skin and think from his or her perspective.

But God can do that. He understands us with perfect accuracy (1 Sam. 16:7). He would like us to see things from his point of view (Col. 1:10), and surely he will help us to see objects, events, situations, and people (including ourselves) through the other person's eyes. This can lead to greater understanding—and understanding is of crucial importance if we want to get along with others and care for them effectively.

Working on Communication

Ask any marriage counselor to list the major problems in families today and it is likely you will hear about a lack of communication. We may be walking in a close relationship with Jesus Christ, we honestly may have attempted to evaluate our own faults and harmful attitudes, we sincerely may seek to see a situation from the point of view of another, but it is difficult to care and to get along if we cannot communicate effectively.

Communication demands that we learn to listen without jumping to conclusions and without interrupting. Effective listening requires that we give people our undivided attention and that we patiently give them time to express themselves.

Have you ever noticed, in the heat of an argument, how several people sometimes talk all at once? In our house we have something called "the 30-second rule." If any one of us feels that others are not listening we call for the 30-second rule. That means that everyone else has to keep quiet for at least 30 seconds (sometimes more) until one person has stated his or her message and relinquished the floor to another who then can also talk for 30 seconds without interruption. Everyone in the room has the privilege of making a contribution without interruption, although it sometimes happens that members of the family will "pass" and not take their turn in the conversation. The purpose of this little gimmick is to make sure that others are listening, especially when one person feels hurt or misunderstood.

But even with such communication rules sometimes people still fail to listen. Have you ever heard the conversations of very young children? Sometimes one will talk, then the other will talk but there isn't any real communication because the two children are talking about entirely different issues. They are not listening to each other; they are simply taking turns talking. Too often, I suspect, this is true of adults. We take turns talking, but we don't listen. As a result we don't understand. When we don't understand, it is hard to get along and difficult to care.

Even when we listen, however, communication sometimes does not take place because people do not express themselves explicitly and honestly. We must learn to say clearly what we want, how we feel, or what we observe. We must learn to speak the truth but in an attitude of love which avoids unkind comments, untruths, or emotionally laden words that are likely to bring more reaction than understanding.

It is important, too, that we avoid what psychologists call "double messages." These occur when a person says one thing but communicates something different by posture, attitudes, and actions. A father, for example, might tell his children, "I love you very much," but if he then is highly critical, insensitive, and unwilling to spend time with the family, he is communicating a double message. His words say one thing but his actions say something else.

It is easy to give a double message about caring. With our lips we can tell others how much we care, but all the talking in the world will be meaningless if these words are not followed up by compassionate acts of concern. Almost the entire Book of James deals with this issue of words without actions. When we really care we work to avoid double messages. Our words and our actions are consistent. This lets us be understood and that improves communication.

Caring When Care Isn't Wanted

Caring is a two-way relationship. There has to be at least one person who cares and another person who accepts that care. But because of pride, stubbornness, fear, or other reasons some people are unwilling to accept our care. They resist our attempts to communicate or to understand. They refuse to forgive, and they may not appreciate our attempts to reach out in loving concern.

It is unrealistic to think we are going to get along with everybody, and it is unlikely that we will be able to care for everyone who has a need. In encouraging the Roman Christians to "be at peace with all men" the apostle Paul prefaced his admonition with the phrase, "if possible, so far as it depends on you" (Rom. 12:18). This seems to indicate that sometimes people will not be able to live together in harmony. There may be times when we must accept the existence of disagreements or divisions, do what we can to resolve them, and then get along as best we can even though the conflicts may persist.

On other occasions it may be that we should withdraw. Apparently there were individuals in the early church who were creating dissension by teaching things about Christ which were not true. These troublemakers were persuasive but basically self-centered. The apostle's advice for dealing with such people was pretty simple: avoid them, especially if such people are causing dissension because of faulty doctrine (Rom. 16:17, 18; 2 Thess. 3:6).

This does not mean that we should withdraw into our own little groups and wallow in pride because we have been rebuffed in our desires to help—intent on remaining "unspotted by the world" that does not appreciate our help. Such behavior is sinful and disobedient to a God who has commanded us to go into the world to witness by word and deed—even when we are rejected.

There may be another reason why we avoid caring—especially when others don't seem to want or appreciate our help. In our society many people seem to have accepted what Francis Schaeffer calls "the attitudes of personal peace and affluence."

> Personal peace means just to be let alone, not to be troubled by the troubles of other people, whether across the world or across the city—to live one's life with minimal possibilities of being personally disturbed. Personal peace means wanting to have my personal life pattern undisturbed in my lifetime, regardless of what the result will be in the lifetimes of my children and grandchildren. Affluence means an overwhelming and ever-increasing prosperity—a life made up of things, things, and more things—a success judged by an ever-higher level of material abundance. . . . In both international and home affairs, expediency—at any price to maintain personal peace and affluence at the moment—is the accepted procedure.[4]

In urbanized communities especially, we each like to do our own thing, to "look out for number one," to complain that "It's their own fault so I don't need to help," or to pass by other people assuming that "they'll get along O.K. without me" since "somebody else probably will come along and help."

Recently our family was driving down a busy street in a Chicago suburb when one of us noticed a man lying in the snow. He appeared to be wearing a jogging suit and it was suggested that perhaps he had stopped for a rest. We had driven almost two blocks before agreeing that even joggers aren't likely to rest in a snowbank at the edge of a sidewalk. As I changed lanes and prepared to go back, one of the children protested that a return would not be safe. "What if the man is a robber?" she asked. "What if he is lying in the snow trying to trick somebody into stopping?"

It was at that time when we spotted a police car and were able to inform the policeman of what we had seen. He drove off to investigate—and as we continued on our way we had an interesting discussion of the good Samaritan.

Perhaps most people remember that story of the man who was robbed, stripped, beaten, and left to lie at the side of the road. Two people passed him by but a third, someone of a different land, picked him up, bandaged his wounds, took him to a place of rest, and even paid for his lodging and recuperation. When Jesus told that story (Luke 10:30–37), he told his followers to "Go and do the same." But how easy it is to find logical reasons for not becoming involved.

We Christians have no biblical or other reason for isolating ourselves from needy people. With an attitude of respect for those who do not want our help, we should continue to pray for others, to not speak against one another, to serve others, and to reach out to one another consistently and lovingly.

Caring—One at a Time

Most of us have had the experience of reading articles or listening to speakers who dramatically picture human needs and then challenge us to reach out in ways that will eliminate injustice or change the world. Such pleas can arouse considerable guilt followed by frustration because there seems so little any one person can really do.

Remember, however, that none of us has a responsibility to care for the whole world. Instead, our task is to care for the people who are closest to us. In this way we care for the world by starting with individuals, one at a time.

This is exactly what Jesus did. At times, of course, he preached to the crowds and he even fed thousands of people, but more often he touched lives one at a time and cared for people in little groups. He entrusted his whole ministry to a small band of fallible individuals who went out to change the world and turn it upside down, often by reaching one person at a time. The readers of this book can do the same. If each of us determines to be more caring, we can reach out in acts of compassion, one at a time, just as Jesus demonstrated and commanded.

8

Caring about Our Families

NOT LONG AGO I arrived for a conference in a distant city and was met by a lady who apparently decided that the trip from the airport would be a good opportunity for us to talk about a personal problem in her own marriage. In some detail she told about her husband, a man who was a committed Christian, actively involved in personal evangelism, and sincerely concerned about caring for other people. Almost every evening, the lady reported, her husband was out counseling with someone who had a need. On the night before my arrival, for example, he had called his wife from work to say that he probably would not be home until after midnight because of his concern for a mutual acquaintance who was having problems and needed help.

"When I hung up the phone," the lady reported, "I cried. But I really wanted to shout: 'Has it never occurred to you that I needed to be cared for too?'"

Apparently there was no reason to believe that the husband was being unfaithful, and the woman denied that there were any other tensions in the marriage. She was angry, however, because she had a husband who was available to care for everyone except the members of his own family.

This is not an isolated incident. At times, perhaps, it happens to all of us. Impressed by the needs around us and sincerely wanting to help, we overlook the needs in our own families. Sometimes, without even being aware of what we are doing, we leave our own family members to care for themselves while we run around caring for others. As a result, resentments build up in the home and these can be followed by emotional outbursts which drive the family further apart. Individual family members begin to spend more time outside the home and the situation inside the household deteriorates further.

Sometimes this happens in the homes of pastors where the demands of a ministry slowly erode away any time with the family. I saw it once in the life of a physician who became so involved in caring for his patients that the family deteriorated and his marriage ended in divorce. There are times when I can see a similar tendency in myself. It is easy to get so involved in speaking and writing books (even about caring) that family discipline is left to my wife, less and less time is spent in family activities, and we begin to wonder why there is a tension build-up at home. Often my wife sees this developing before I do, and when she points it out, I try to change quickly. This involves reevaluating my priorities, trimming down some of my outside activities, and spending more time with the family.

Such changes are not always easy, especially for the family breadwinner. Most of our income and social status comes from the things we do away from home, but it is good to remember that there is nothing more devastating and pathetic than a dedicated Christian who has become so concerned in caring for other people that he or she has forgotten the family and lost the respect of people at home. It is in our own homes that we should be most diligent about applying the caring principles elaborated in this book.

The Family in Trouble

When God created human beings he put us in families and gave us some guidelines on how we ought to get along with each other. Created even before the church, the family is so important that it is mentioned in all 66 books of the Bible.

One need not be an expert to know that families have been undergoing radical changes within recent years. The divorce rate is increasing, there is confusion over roles, families are torn apart by frequent moves, and instead of being the traditional place of refuge, many homes have become storm centers. Rather than being a place where people come for love, support, and growth, numerous families have become centers of conflict—little more than a rest stop where relatives come to eat, to sleep (sometimes), and to do their laundry before rushing off to another event or activity outside the home.

Within recent years many remedies have been proposed for increasing family unity and stability. There are university study centers to analyze the family, counseling centers to help the family, conferences to professionally discuss the family, and numerous seminars, books, and magazine articles which tell us how to care about the family. Thousands of perceptive, well-meaning people—including family members—are trying to find out why the family is in trouble and what can be done about it.

Why is the family in trouble? One reason is that our society is changing—so quickly, in fact, that the family does not know how to keep up. Consider, for example, the issue of mobility. People move so frequently and so far that we no longer have parents, grandparents, aunts, uncles, cousins, and other family members nearby to enjoy each other and help in times of need. Very often, relationships with the neighbors are kept on a superficial level so the pain of separation won't be so great when it comes time for someone to move. In addition, there is much more community tolerance for divorce, working mothers, couples not having children, and other life styles which affect family stability. Perhaps an even greater social change has been the tendency for almost every traditional task of the family to pass out of the home and into the hands of schools, governments, professional providers, and even the church.

The family now looks outside the home for advice or help and some of the traditional reasons for family togetherness no longer exist.

The influence of the mass media, especially television, has also affected the family. In some homes television has become the major babysitter, a dispenser of values, and the center of attention which replaces family recreation, conversation, and worship.

Another problem for the family is the sheer cost of raising children, paying the mortgage, and meeting the expenses of education, recreation, and taxation. Increasing financial strain can put great pressure on family stability.

In light of these issues, many parents and family members may feel that they will never be able to succeed in building a successful marriage or in raising healthy, normal children. It is easy to feel overwhelmed by the influence of television, schools, and peer groups. Also, it is frustrating to face a conflict between the modern idea that individuals should seek personal fulfillment and the old idea that family members should work together. When we look to professionals for advice we discover that some of the most prominent advice-givers have unruly children and problems with their own marriages. Little wonder that so many people give up, watch their families disintegrate, and then try again!

Caring for the Family

In caring it is important to remember that the family is still the basic unit of society. God has never declared it obsolete, even with its problems. Within its setting, individual family members can learn to care for each other so that they, in turn, can care for the people who live in the community and in the world outside the home.

How do we care for our families? There are several answers:

The family, for example, should be a top order of priority in our lives. This is especially true for fathers and husbands who have a tendency to get caught up on their work and leave the family problems to someone else—most often the mother.

Do you care about your family enough to spend time with them (even when it is inconvenient)? Do you care enough to give your energy and your attention (even when you would much prefer to be doing something else)? If God has placed us in families he clearly expects us to be good parents, children, husbands, and wives—every bit as much as (probably more than) he expects us to be good church members, employees, or members of the community. When I get to heaven I expect God will ask me to give an account for the writing and speaking responsibilities he has given to me, but I suspect that he might be equally concerned about my stewardship as a husband, father, and family member. That is a sobering realization for any follower of Jesus Christ.

There is something inconsistent about wanting to care for people outside the home but not taking the time or effort to care for the needy people with whom we live. Caring for our families, therefore, should be a high priority item in our lives.

In addition, *we should seek to follow biblical guidelines for family life.* God, who created us, knows us intimately. He instituted marriage and laid out a family plan which is recorded in the Bible and summarized succinctly in Colossians 3 (verses 18–21, NIV):

> Wives, submit to your husbands, as is fitting in the Lord.
> Husbands, love your wives and do not be harsh with them.
> Children, obey your parents in everything, for this pleases the Lord.
> Fathers, do not embitter your children, or they will become discouraged.

Some people have criticized these verses, suggesting that this "puts down" women, but you will notice that this in no way implies the inferiority of women; neither does it imply that they are nonthinking, tied to housework, or of lesser

importance than men. All family members are to be subject
to one another (Eph. 5:21), but the husband has the major
responsibility for the home. He is to love his wife as Christ
loved us—with no strings attached. The husband is to love
his wife unselfishly, as he loves his own body. He is required
to help the children obey and to discipline them in a way
that does not cause bitterness on their part. The children, in
turn, are expected to be obedient to and honor their
parents. None of this sanctions male or female dominance
or power struggles between family members. It is a plan in
which the family members respect each other and care for
one another.

Regrettably, there is considerable confusion about these
scriptural instructions. Various speakers and writers, while
attempting to be biblical, nevertheless have used the same
verses (in Eph. 5:22–31) to reach different and sometimes
conflicting conclusions. It is important, therefore, that we
attempt to rid our minds of pride or prejudice before
interpreting this passage from the Bible, and that we seek
the Holy Spirit's special guidance in applying these verses to
our own families. Gene Getz has made another observation
which helps with the interpretation of these verses. According to Getz, the Bible really gives very few instructions
about the family.

> Since so many problems in the world—from time imme-
> morial—originate in the home, why hasn't God given us a
> guidebook for the home? Why aren't larger portions of the
> New Testament devoted to this important institution? Why
> hasn't the Lord left us with more direct information and
> instructions?
>
> The fact is, He has! . . . The Christian home in the New
> Testament world was almost synonymous with the Church.
> In reality, an individual household in some instances *was* a
> local church—at least in its initial days. . . . Therefore we
> discover numerous references in the New Testament to
> household churches.
>
> These observations lead us to a very important con-
> clusion. What was written to the Church was also written to
> individual families. Most of the New Testament, then, can
> be applied directly to individual family units. We *do* have a

> guidebook for the family unit! The Church simply becomes an umbrella concept that includes the home. The family is really the *Church in miniature.* True, on occasions the New Testament writers zero in on special needs that are uniquely related to family living. But in the most part, what was written to believers as a whole applies directly to Christians living in the smaller context of the home. . . . Whatever was written to local churches was in essence written to individual family units.[1]

In caring for families, including our own, Christians have the entire teaching of the Bible as a guidebook for living inside the home as well as outside.

The home should be made a place for teaching. When the Israelites were about to enter the Promised Land, God gave the parents, especially the fathers, a three-part formula for instilling spiritual truths in their young people. First, the parents were to listen to the Word of God so they could understand it in their own minds. Second, they were to "do it," obediently loving and serving God with all their heart, soul, and mind. Third, they were to teach their children diligently and in a way which consisted of more than formal instruction. The parents were to talk about spiritual truths "when you sit in your house and when you walk by the way and when you lie down and when you rise up" (Deut. 6:7). Undoubtedly, some of the best opportunities for spiritual teaching come during times when we're riding in the car, pondering a news report, or discussing the day's events around the dinner table. If family members, especially parents, know God's Word and seek to obey it, then they are much more credible when it comes to teaching children to do likewise.

Family caring must allow for flexibility. All of us are aware that we live in a society where there are many influences tugging for our attention and sometimes pulling the family apart. After-school activities, the P.T.A., continuing education classes, community projects, television, church meetings—these and a host of other influences vie for the time of each family member and call both for a flexibility in family routines and for a willingness to juggle family schedules. In addition, we must remember that each person in the family has a unique personality. We have individual differences in level of maturity, interests, and sometimes in our values. Our task in the family, therefore, is not to reform each other but to help each other grow and to develop each person's individual potential within the guidelines of Scripture.

For many years professional counselors tended to focus their attention on the problems of individuals. More recently, however, a new movement has arisen in the mental health field. Since most people live within a family setting there now is a tendency to treat not just the individual who most clearly demonstrates a problem but to treat the entire family. The emphasis is on teaching family members how to get along with each other, how to understand each other, and how to support, encourage, and communicate with one another. All of this stimulates flexibility and that brings more effective caring.

The family must learn to communicate. Failure to communicate clearly, a problem which is at the basis of so many interpersonal problems, comes up with special clarity in the family. All of the rules for good communication—learning to listen, expressing ourselves clearly, openly acknowledging our real feelings, speaking the truth in love—apply to the family situation. Misunderstandings, failure to listen, not saying what we really mean—these and other common communication problems frequently create misunderstanding and often lead to conflict within family settings. Raised in a society which emphasizes self-centeredness, the husband, wife, and subsequently the other family members often slip into a mentality where each person attempts to dominate and to get his or her own way at the expense of others in the family.

Of course some families have deteriorated so much that family members must protect themselves to survive psychologically if not physically. Nevertheless, complete self-centeredness is a characteristic of immaturity. Whenever we are determined primarily to get what we can for ourselves without being concerned about others, we have slipped into a way of thinking which ultimately ruins the family and is self-destructive. When signs of such self-centeredness appear, those families who can do so should sit down and talk about what is happening. Others may want to seek the counsel of a pastor or family therapist who can help the family members understand each other and communicate more effectively.

One way to do this is to learn the act of giving and to develop the art of loving. Too often in the home, we are more concerned about what we can get than about what we can give to other people. If our marriages and our families are to grow we must be willing to give time, energy, interest, consideration, creative ideas, and especially love.

More than any other person in the history of the world, Jesus Christ demonstrated love. He showed us a love that is completely patient, kind, gentle, and unselfish. Such a love does not spring up spontaneously; neither is it primarily something we feel. When we commit our lives to Christ, his love is available to flow through us and out to other people. We begin by doing loving actions, realizing that loving feelings come along later. When we learn to show loving actions at home, our families become more and more like the caring institutions God originally intended them to be.

We must reach out to other families. Several years ago over 2,000 Christian leaders gathered in St. Louis, Missouri, for a week-long Continental Congress on the Family. During the convention, a statement was prepared to express concern about the status of the family and to summarize the Bible's teachings on family life and related issues. One of the segments in this "affirmation on the family" concerned the Christian family in the church. Its somewhat formal language read as follows:

> The family as a unit is not self-sufficient and self-contained as a body of believers. Rather, the family has need of continuing support from other families and from individuals within the Body. The local Church is a company

of believers who exist for fellowship, worship, teaching, and the development of spiritual gifts to the end that God will be glorified and the Body of Christ edified. As part of the universal Body of Christ, the local Church is an extended family composed of individual families. The Church exists to support, nurture, and equip individuals and families for growth in discipleship (including evangelism) and effective functioning. We urge, therefore, that families become involved actively in the local Church and that they pray, worship, and serve Christ together. We urge churches to minister to families and individuals in creative ways which build Church and family unity, prepare people for mate selection and marriage, educate families in effective family living, assist family members and individuals in their spiritual and personal growth, and give support in times of stress or special need.[2]

Some family life experts are now beginning to realize that families need other families. When families live together in small communities they help each other by nourishing, encouraging, and supporting one another. However, in our urban societies we seem to have concluded that families, like individuals, can succeed on their own. As a result we have failed to acknowledge that just as individuals must bear one another's burdens, so must families help, nurture, and equip each other. This can be done in the neighborhood and apartment complexes where many of us live, but it must also be done in the local church where families worship and serve together with other families.

The local church body should also recognize that many people today do not live in traditional family settings. In addition to widows, widowers, and never-married adults, there are increasing numbers of separated and divorced people in our society, many of whom are parents without partners. These people need to feel that they are accepted as equal members within the family of believers which comprises the local church. Single people and married people need each other in the same way that the old need the young, the young need the old, and people at different levels of maturity need and can help one another.

I once had a friend who decided his family had no goals except for some vague hopes that "we would all get along" or that "the children would grow up into well-rounded people." One day the family sat down and decided together on their long-range and short-term goals for the future. Once they had their goals in mind they were able to plan specific ways in which they could reach these goals. This created a significant increase in family unity and cohesiveness.

What are the goals for your marriage and your family? What are some ways of reaching these goals? What are some projects you can do together, some ways in which you can give the family a higher order of priority, some techniques for building solid relationships that are consistent with biblical teaching?

All of our discussions on caring are largely meaningless if we have not learned to care for the people with whom we live. It isn't always easy to show compassion at home. But it is at home that we begin to experience the real joy of caring. And it is from the home that we can reach out to care for others in the community.

9

Caring about Our Communities

IN THE WINTER of 1944, a few days before the beginning of the new year, the massive gates of Ravensbruck Nazi prison camp slammed shut, discharging the physically weakened and psychologically drained body of a middle-aged woman named Corrie ten Boom.

Miss ten Boom had grown up in Holland where she had worked with her father and sister in the family jewelry shop. When the Nazi armies swept across Europe, toppling governments, persecuting civilians, and attempting to liquidate Jews, the ten Boom family slowly became part of the underground resistance movement. Believing it was their Christian duty to help persecuted Jews, the ten Booms made their home a hiding place, where fearful and fleeing individuals could find rest and protection in a time of suffering and persecution. Eventually the ten Booms were arrested. The aged father died after only a few days in jail, and his daughter Betsie died following several months in the lice-infested prison.

Almost a year after the arrest, Corrie found herself released into the cold winter weather, without money, without friends, and in the middle of war-torn Germany. Slowly, she made her way back to Holland and soon was involved in helping people who, like herself, had suffered during the war. The ten Boom family had been arrested because of their care for needy people; caring was part of their life style. Before the war they each had been actively concerned with helping the needy and no sooner had Corrie been released from prison than she began reaching out again, caring for people, and showing them God's love by her actions and by her words. She began to speak of her experiences and in later years traveled all around the world telling people about the God who had sustained her during the prison ordeal. She spoke, too, of her sister Betsie who had dreamed of helping needy people after the war. Shortly before her death Betsie had expressed the hope of being able to "tell people what we have learned here. We must tell them," she had said, that "there is no pit so deep that He is not deeper still. They will listen to us, Corrie, because we have been here."

Many years have passed since World War II, and the cruelty of the Nazis is remembered only by those who today are middle-aged or older. It is easy, perhaps, to read about Corrie ten Boom, to admire her courage, and then to dismiss her story as being irrelevant for the age in which we live. But in some parts of the world people today are suffering, even as Corrie suffered, and could it be that some readers of this book, perhaps you, might be called upon to suffer intensely in the future?

In comparison with less developed parts of the world and with other periods of history most readers of this book live in relative comfort. But we also live in a world that is filled with violence, crime, poverty, pollution, and hunger. Scientists, politicians, and news analysts warn that our natural resources are being wasted, our morals are declining, and our economy is unstable.

Many people close their eyes to all this, expecting that the problems will go away or that some magic solution will be found—perhaps by science or superior statesmanship. Others have slipped into despair, abandoning hope that our world can be diverted from its self-destructive course. Some have determined to destroy the establishment, hoping that something better can arise from the resulting chaos. Still others have sought temporary relief by giving themselves to drugs, Eastern religions, or the mythical predictions of astrology and horoscopes. Then there are those, perhaps the majority, who have devoted their energies to the pursuit of pleasure, status, and their own personal ends. Apparently many of these people can see no way in which, as individuals, they can deal with the complex and overwhelming problems of the world in which we live. What is more distressing is that some people don't even seem to care. But Jesus took a different view. He was actively concerned about the poverty, immorality, and social injustice of his society. After instructing us to love our neighbor, he told the story of a good Samaritan who, unlike some religious people, stopped to care for a stranger in need. The man who helped "showed mercy," Jesus said, and we Christians must "Go and do the same" (Luke 10:37), no matter how hopeless this may seem.

The former editor of *Decision* magazine wrote about this concisely several years ago:

> The typical Gospel church of our day is not the fundamentalist enclave it was at the turn of the century. Its congregation still wants its minister to be fervent, dedicated, evangelistic and Biblically oriented, but a new element has entered the picture. Today's evangelical congregation wishes its pastor also to be imaginatively and effectively cognizant of the social ferment going on about him. It does not want him taking political sides, but it wants him socially sensitive to all sides. It wants his prayers to reflect the truth that God is in the world as well as in the church. It wants his sermons to give out equipment for dealing with the "space age" in the mode of the living Christ. Some evangelical seminaries have forged ahead of the congregations in the matter. Without forsaking the spiritual heritage of the faith, without reducing the content of the Bible, they are implanting in their men and women students the conviction that the Christian, because he is a member of the human race, has inescapable responsibilities to society.[1]

In a time when the problems of society appear to be getting worse, instead of better, Christians have a God-given privilege and responsibility both to point individuals to Christ and to work at improving our world. This is true caring and what makes it especially exciting is this comment of Jesus: "to the extent that you did it to one of these brothers of Mine, even the least of them, you did it to Me" (Matt. 25:40).[2]

How do we help a world in need? We can learn to understand community needs more accurately, we can become involved with needy individuals, we can give special care to people in times of crisis, and we can share the good news that the Word of God has practical relevance to those who are in need of care. Let us consider each of these in more detail.

Knowing the Situation

In the late 1960s, when political, social, and student unrest were at their height, one writer suggested that the first step to practical action is to "read, baby, read."[3] No scientist ever begins research without becoming familiar with everything written about the problem to be studied. While such scientific rigor does not need to characterize people whose prime concern is to help others in the community, there is considerable value in learning all we can about the needs in our communities. Regretfully, there are many well-meaning but ill-informed "do gooders" who sincerely want to help but who sometimes make matters worse because they do not understand the needs of their community.

At one time in my life I was invited to teach counseling on the campus of a university situated in the inner city of a large metropolitan area. The campus was surrounded by ghettos, and many of my students were black. During that year I think I learned more from the students than they did from me. One of the things they complained about, and rightly so, was the tendency of well-meaning people who came from the suburbs to "help the poor blacks in the city" without realizing how the people in the inner city really felt.

Such efforts at helping were doomed to failure right from the beginning because many of the helpers had not taken the time to learn about the real needs and frustrations of the people in the ghettos. Listening to people's needs, reading articles and books, and keeping abreast of the news can all enable us to be more aware of the needs in our communities. Government publications and newsletters from politicians are often informative and availab e free if we ask. Local charities and religious groups can also alert us to community, national, and international ne d_o. Such familiarity will alert us to paths through which we can care in more practical ways.

Daily Involvement

Part of the frustration which many of us feel in our desire to care for the community is that we do not know specifically what we can do. As individuals how can we stop crime, end war, eliminate poverty, feed the hungry, halt drug traffic, clean up polluted lakes, bring efficiency to government, or eliminate social injustice? Little wonder that we give up in despair.

A story was told about a pasture open to herdsmen for grazing their cattle. For many centuries tribal wars and disease kept the number of both men and beasts well below the capacity of the land, but one day social stability came to the country and each of the herdsmen was free to direct his attention to the goal of increasing his herd. To increase profits each herdsman had to ask, "Would there be anything wrong if I added one more animal to the herd? Certainly," each concluded, "with all this land one more animal wouldn't make any difference." So each herdsman added another animal, then another, and before long each man was locked into a system of increasing his possessions and pursuing his own best interests at the expense of a society which to that point had encouraged freedom in the pasture. Eventually, however, the herdsmen ran out of grazing land, their herds had nothing to eat, and everyone was ruined.[4]

In a reverse way, the same tragedy occurs with pollution. Here the problem is not that of taking natural resources out of the world but of putting something in—sewage into the water, fumes into the atmosphere, noise into the air. No one person pollutes the whole environment, just as no one person creates an energy shortage, but each of us in a small way contributes to the problems of the society. The world population grows because husbands and wives do not limit the size of their families; hostility increases because we let children watch television violence indiscriminately; injustice flourishes because individuals remain silent; highway tragedies continue because people overlook speed limits; pollution is worse because suburbanites drive big cars instead of using smaller vehicles or mass transportation.

Before God, each of us must ask, "Am I by my actions and inactions contributing to the worsening state of society? Am I ignoring people in need and continuing with my own self-centered interests?" Each of us is only one person and of course it is unrealistic to assume that everyone else will voluntarily act in ways that will be good for others. But Jesus expects us to be servants (Matt. 20:26, 27) compassionately reaching out one by one to others. We are responsible to do what we can to care for and clean up the environment and society—even if everyone else appears to ignore the needs and be caught up in self-centered pursuits.

Most people who make a lasting impact on society probably do not set out to change the world by mass movements—helpful as these may be at times. Most begin in their own neighborhoods and communities, helping people, including strangers, in times of need, and doing what they can to improve the lot of mankind. As we have mentioned in a previous chapter, this was the way Jesus helped: reaching out to one person at a time, day by day.

Periodically, we read newspaper accounts that tell how people have been beaten or injured but who have received no help from passersby. Why do people not stop to help a stranded motorist or to assist someone with a physical problem?

Some psychologists once decided to study this and concluded that several conditions must be met before an onlooker helps.[5] First, the onlooker must notice that something is wrong. Caught up in our busy activities and reluctant to stare at people, we often ignore individuals under stress and don't even notice when they have a need.

But even if we do notice, we don't help unless we conclude that there is an emergency. If we conclude that the problem is not an emergency, we go on our way without getting involved. This is likely to happen especially when other people are rushing on by with us. If everyone else is passing someone in need, we conclude that apparently there really isn't any emergency which needs our help. Certainly, none of us wants to look like a fool reaching out to help people when help isn't needed.

Even if we notice a situation, and decide that there is an emergency, there is still another decision to be made before we act to help. We must decide that it is our responsibility to intervene and not the responsibility of someone else. Several years ago, a New York woman was murdered in the courtyard of her apartment while 38 neighbors watched from their windows. Not one of them called the police. When they were interviewed later, each of these people had noticed the situation, each realized that it was an emergency, but each assumed that someone else had called the police. As a result, no one acted, the police were not summoned, the woman died, and her murderer escaped.

Have you ever noticed how these three steps—noticing a problem, deciding there is a need, and taking responsibility—are involved even in little acts of caring? How many people have visited churches where no one spoke to them and where the atmosphere radiated that the other worshipers were decidedly unfriendly toward strangers? It is easy for regular church members not to notice someone new. Even if we notice, we may decide that the stranger "probably is somebody who is here all the time—and it would be stupid to speak to someone who might attend as often as I do." Suppose, however, that we decide the visitor *is* a stranger. Often we then conclude that greeting newcomers is someone else's responsibility, so we gravitate to our friends and trust that some usher will shake the visitor's hand on the way out the door.

Jesus noticed the people around him, he was alert to their needs, and he was not reluctant to reach out and help the individuals whom he met. As followers of Jesus Christ, we have a responsibility to do likewise.

Caring in Crisis

During his years of ministry on earth, Jesus traveled a great deal but apparently he found frequent refuge in the home of Mary, Martha, and Lazarus of Bethany. As almost every child learns in Sunday school, Lazarus became very ill on one occasion, died, and was buried—all while Jesus was in another part of the country.

The funeral was over when Christ chose to return to Bethany where he found a scene of great mourning. The disciples were confused because Jesus had not healed Lazarus, and the neighbors were critical for the same reason. Mary and Martha, even though comforted by their belief in the resurrection of the dead, nevertheless were very sad and in tears when Jesus arrived.

As he surveyed the scene, Jesus was so moved with compassion that he cried. He knew that Lazarus was about to be raised from the dead, he knew that God and his Son were about to be "glorified" by this event and that people would believe in Christ if they saw God's power over death; nevertheless Jesus was sad along with the mourners, so much so that he wept.

It is difficult to help people when they are in times of crisis. Even though we are certain of God's sovereign working in all of human affairs, we often feel helpless when we stand with the grieving, the dying, or those who suffer. At times we might even wish that someone else could take over the difficult task of caring—but others cannot always be present. People in crisis most frequently turn to neighbors, relatives, friends, and others who are nearby. It is these lay people who must encourage, listen to the expression of feelings, give an objective perspective on the situation, instill hope, and bring comfort.

One writer has suggested that people in crisis can be helped by the application of an ABC approach.[6]

A—Achieve contact. This involves going to people in crisis wherever they are. It involves showing warmth and concern, and encouraging people to talk about the crisis, assuring them of your desire to stick with them in times of need, and building up at least a ray of hope about the future.

B—Boil down the problem. It is helpful if people can get a clear perspective on what really is putting them under pressure and what they can and cannot do next.

C—Cope actively with the problem. Here we can help people evaluate what they have done to solve the problem in the past and think realistically about what may or may not work in the future. Then we can encourage them to take action, we can stick with them, and we can help them reevaluate their actions, especially if these actions fail to bring the desired results.

In crisis intervention there are three important facts to remember. First, it is God who heals and ultimately helps. He has the power to do this instantly, to remove crises and to bring immediate recovery. But more often he works through imperfect human instruments to accomplish his purposes. Surely, therefore, the caring helper will be more effective if he or she is a praying helper who is familiar with the Scriptures and available to be used by the Holy Spirit to bring help and healing.

Second, we must never overlook the importance of the Body as a healing community. When we are in the midst of a crisis (and even when there is no crisis) we need one another. Caring is most effective and growth is most healthy when we are part of a group where Christians support, encourage, guide, pray for, accept, forgive, build up, serve, love, and bear the burdens of one another. The caring community of believers can be a powerful force not only for healing but for preventing problems which might otherwise develop.

Third, remember that there will be failures in the midst of our successes. Some people face a crisis and experience the pain or sadness, but are able—in time and with the help of God and other people—to readjust, to go on living a satisfying life, and to mature as a result of their crisis. For these people a crisis is a growing experience.

For others, however, there is no growth. Even in spite of prayers and personal counseling some people retreat in the face of a crisis. They grow worse instead of better and sometimes show increasing depression, self-condemnation, bitterness, withdrawal, or self-pity. At times there is excessive drinking, dependence on drugs, or the development of various physical problems.

What can we do when people respond in this way to a crisis? As a beginning, do not give up too quickly. At times suffering people become worse before they get better and in such cases they are not helped when they are abandoned early as hopeless cases. Continue to apply the ABC approach, bathed in prayer and bolstered by a loving concern from members of the body of Christ—including you. If matters still do not improve, encourage the person to get a physical examination to determine if there is a physical basis for the problem. Then you might suggest that the person seek out a capable professional counselor who might be able to help bring about improvement.

In Bethany the results were different. Jesus showed a deep compassion for the mourners at Lazarus' grave. He prayed in their presence and was used by God to turn their sorrow into rejoicing. As a result of his caring actions, Jesus came under excessive criticism and some of the religious leaders determined to kill him. But others believed, their faith was strengthened, and they grew personally and spiritually (John 11:1–54). We may stimulate similar negative reactions from people today when we dare to help in a crisis. But there also can be encouragement and joy when we reach out to care whenever crises come to individuals and families in our communities.

Sharing the Good News

Probably the most quoted verse in the Bible is John 3:16: "For God so loved the world, that He gave His only begotten Son, that whoever believes in Him should not perish, but have eternal life." The Bible also states that anyone who believes in Jesus Christ is not judged as are those who do not believe and are condemned because of individual sin. There is no condemnation for those who are in Christ Jesus (Rom. 8:1)—for those who have confessed their sin and acknowledged the Lordship of Jesus Christ. Such people have real inner peace even in the midst of tribulation (Rom. 5:1–3).

There was a time, not many years ago, when many Christians who accepted the authority of the Bible preached that all of us are sinners in need of a Savior, encouraged individuals to put their faith in Jesus Christ, and then ignored the personal and psychological needs of people, especially nonbelievers. Other believers, however, went the other way. They overemphasized society's needs and showed little concern for the salvation of individuals. But the proclamation of the gospel and its outward demonstration are both clearly taught in the Bible. We can't have one without the other. Faith in Jesus Christ as Savior and Lord is dead and meaningless if such faith does not lead us to love our neighbor as we love ourselves (James 3:8, 9; Mark 12:29–31). Love and concern for our neighbor are futile if we are not at the same time burdened about his or her personal relationship with Jesus Christ.

Jesus commanded his followers to teach what he taught, and this includes social concern, but he also told us to preach so that individuals who believe will be saved from an empty, miserable life without Christ after death (Matt.

28:19; Mark 16:16). To spread this message and to care in a practical way is the double responsibility of every believer.

As people around us suffer and the problems of society seem so unsolvable, it is easy to panic, to retreat in fear, or to give up in discouragement. But this cannot be the reaction of a true follower of Jesus Christ! Christians know for certain that he who created all things is still sovereign and in control, holding the world together by his power (Col. 1:16, 17; Heb. 1:1, 2). Such a realization should spur us on to action as good and faithful servants who are concerned about using our God-given talents as Christ has commanded. We need not lose hope because we know that God can redeem any situation. In contrast, we need not commit ourselves to utopian schemes, and neither do we gullibly accept the optimistic statements of public figures because we know that all are sinners and that human failure is common. We also know that God uses individuals to achieve his purposes and because of this we continue to "plug away," obediently recognizing that as followers of Christ we must be involved in whatever way possible to help people in the community and in the world where we live.

As Christians, we have a God-given privilege and responsibility to point individuals to Jesus Christ. What about you? Have you committed your life to Jesus Christ in prayer asking him to forgive your sins, guide your life, and meet your needs? Have you an interest in telling this good news to others?

Then as Christians we have a responsibility for improving our world in whatever way we can. Do you have such a commitment? To be a follower of Jesus Christ clearly implies that we will be caring for other people whenever and wherever possible.

10
Caring about Our Leaders

When I was a boy we periodically would have special meetings at our church in which some outside speaker, sometimes accompanied by a musician, would come for evangelistic or spiritual life meetings. Often these were high points in my life. I was impressed by the music, edified by the messages, and often caught up on the emotional swell of the services. As a high school student, I decided that I would like to become one of these itinerant speakers, moving from town to town, swaying crowds by the sheer power of my words, and accepting the accolades of grateful and admiring church members.

At the time I knew nothing about the emotional drain, the long separations from family, the struggles with pride and discouragement, the fear of failure, the temptations which come with special intensity when one is alone, or the hard work which faces any person who is "on the road." At that time I knew nothing about the need for every Christian, including speakers and musicians, to depend daily on the power of the Holy Spirit. I did not know that all of us should encourage and pray for those people whose ministry takes them from place to place. It never occurred to me that their God-given work might be far less glamorous than one would think. And I failed to realize the extent to which outsiders so frequently are held in awe.

Have you ever noticed how often we look to visiting speakers for help, encouragement, and instruction? We enjoy outsiders who come to town for a seminar or series of meetings, give us guidelines for living, sometimes promise instant success, and then leave without giving us the opportunity to see whether the teachings really work in people's lives. It is relatively easy to impress people when one flies into town, speaks once or twice from a public platform, and then hurries back to the airport. It is possible for an author to gain a reputation by sitting alone in a room putting words on paper, and knowing that he or she will never be seen by most readers. But when a man or woman comes alone to conduct marriage enrichment seminars, can we be sure that this person has a good marriage back home? When someone writes, talks, or sings about loneliness or discouragement, can we know that the one who communicates really has victory over these common problems? Teaching can be difficult; living what we teach can be harder. It isn't easy to live in the family, to be part of a community, and to teach in school where students can watch week after week. In such situations what Christian leaders tell people is much less important than what they show by their lives.

Sometimes the local ministers appear to be lackluster and dull in comparison to the attractive strangers who pass through our communities. The pastor, however, has the difficult job both of preaching or teaching, and then of living where all can see whether the words of a message actually work in the life of the speaker. Those leaders who sincerely try to preach, teach, and live consistently according to scriptural principles find that consistency is difficult. At times there will be failure, and always there is need for support and caring from others within the body of Christ.

Caring for Spiritual Leaders

Dr. Stuart Briscoe, pastor of a large and growing church in Wisconsin, once told a graduating class of seminarians about some of the pressures in the ministry. There is, he suggested, *congregational pressure*. This comes when church members try to manipulate a pastor, when they antagonize him and try to undercut his work, or when they praise him so much so that he begins to forget his calling and "play up" to the people who think he is so great. Then there is *social pressure* which comes sometimes as criticism because the pastor has dared to challenge secular society and sometimes as praise when a church starts attracting community attention and the pastor finds himself seeking publicity or "doing what the media wants." *Personal pressure* comes when the pastor is so idealistic and unrealistic that he attempts to do everything demanded of him.

To this list we might add that many Christian leaders encounter:

Excessive demands in which a pastor is expected to be a preacher, evangelist, youth leader, janitor, scholar, husband, father, counselor, parish promoter, and community problem solver—to name a few. His wife, who often has had little or no theological training, is frequently expected to speak, to attend meetings, and sometimes fulfill the functions of an assistant pastor. Even the pastor's children are expected to be well-behaved, strongly spiritual, and present at all meetings of their age group. Such demands can rob the pastor's family of time with God, interfere with family fellowship, and bring feelings of anxiety, discouragement, or inferiority when there is criticism or when things are not running smoothly.

Social isolation comes to all people who live in the public eye. The pastor and his wife are often watched critically by the congregation. They must listen to the problems of others since this is an important part of their ministry, but there are few human ears to whom they can confidently express their own discouragements and uncertainties.

Financial strain comes to many whose salaries are low in comparison to other professionals and sometimes well below the average income of the congregation. Added benefits like a free parsonage and housing allowance do not always solve the pastor's financial problems—and do nothing to build equity for the future.

Administrative pressures come because the pastor, who often has little training in good business methods, nevertheless is called upon to be in charge of a large budget, a detailed program, and a church board which is not always sympathetic or supportive. Increasing frustration develops when those who feel called to minister spend large portions of their time performing administrative duties instead.

Professional competition is characteristic of our way of life and, not surprisingly, seeps into the ministry. Large building programs, big churches, expanding membership lists, great crowds, big budgets, or a large number of "decisions," all become status symbols and objects of competition among some pastors. Denominational meetings can be characterized by striving between factions, and this often leads to tension in the lives of the competitors or their families.

Psychological tensions include such things as discouragement, anxiety, anger when things are not going right, feelings of inadequacy, and sometimes guilt over temptations and failures.

It is difficult for any of us to deal with such pressures but this is especially so if we sense that we are failing "in God's work." The Christian leader cannot always share these pressures with others lest people misunderstand or question his or her reasons for talking. We who are church members should recognize, therefore, that our spiritual leaders—who so often give themselves in caring for others—also need to be cared for in return. There are several ways in which this can be done.

For example, we can show *understanding.* Have you ever noticed how often we take our church leaders for granted, slipping into criticism and sitting back expecting that they will do most of the work? To be aware of the pressures of the ministry, to develop an understanding attitude, and to periodically express a word of encouragement are all small but significant ways in which we can care for the individuals who minister to us on a week-to-week basis.

Then we can show *respect*. Do you remember the time when Jesus healed ten men but only one returned to thank him? Have you wondered how he must have felt as he asked what had happened to the other nine?

Like all of us, church leaders need to know that they are appreciated. The apostle Paul wrote about this in strong but compassionate terms when he instructed believers to "encourage one another, and build up one another. . . . We request of you, brethren, that you appreciate those who diligently labor among you, and have charge over you in the Lord and give you instruction, and that you esteem them very highly in love because of their work" (1 Thess. 5:11–13).

It is easy to encourage and respect a church leader when we feel sincere appreciation, but what if we don't respect our leaders? What if we think the pastor is lazy, hypocritical, or inclined to be manipulative? First, it is helpful to remember that some of our criticisms may be unjustified or built on faulty information. After considering this possibility and after prayer, there could be value in going privately to the Christian leader and sharing your concerns in the spirit of love and openness. If he or she refuses to listen then you might consider returning with two or three other Christians who share your concerns, and if there still is no change then you can bring it before the church.

Notice, however, that this biblical procedure is given for dealing with a brother who sins (Matt. 17:15–17). It is not set forth as a procedure for dealing with personality conflicts or differences of opinion. Perhaps it is also interesting to notice that the apostle Paul, after instructing believers to appreciate their leaders, goes on to "urge [that Christians] admonish the unruly, encourage the fainthearted, help the weak, be patient with all men" (1 Thess. 5:14). Perhaps if we can learn to encourage, to help, and to be patient, there will be much less need to admonish or to criticize.

Next, we help our leaders through *prayer*. It is well-known that the apostle Paul was a man of prayer. He begins many of the New Testament epistles with prayer for the readers and he encourages these readers, in turn, to pray for him and for people who are in authority.

The New Testament contains many examples of the power of prayer. This power is still available, and the pastor who is backed by a praying congregation will have a more efficient and spiritually enriched ministry (Eph. 6:18, 19; 1 Thess. 5:17; Col. 4:2).

Do you ever pray for your pastor? Do you pray for Christian leaders in your church, for missionaries, for Christian writers, and for others who have special Christian ministries? Prayer is not only a way of caring, but it also helps us to understand and to be more tolerant of people with whom we might disagree.

Encouragement is another way to care for a church leader. Not long ago a Christian layman wrote the following letter:

> Some months ago I was asked to speak to a group of laymen. I was supposed to speak about the love of Christ which I tried to share to the best of my ability. Somehow I knew, it wasn't enough. There was something else I needed to say, and I couldn't put my finger on it.
>
> I am a builder-contractor. Last year my church asked me to build an education building for the church, which we sorely needed. The new building was to be an extension of the existing structure.
>
> The project went on for four months, and involved close contact with many aspects of church life of which I was completely unaware. It involved directly the pastor's office. What I learned during these four months of daily contact with the pastor, his staff and secretary, have made me a new layman. Never before did I realize just what these people carry on their shoulders.
>
> As time went on I became a fixture, and people who happened in, began to demand certain things from me. Where was the pastor? Why was he not in his office? Why didn't he attend to such and such? When in fact the man was dashing from office, to counselling, to hospital, to mortuary, to board luncheons and visits to homes in trouble. The

telephone never stopped: Worse than in my own office! People came to that little office by droves. People discouraged, unhappy, sorrowing, irate, seeking hope, in need of counselling. Repairmen, office supply people, happy people, sad people, dissatisfied people, Pastor-you-should-know-this people (I know, because they had no inhibitions about telling me), etc., etc.

Because of that four month experience I am absolutely convinced, even though other professions, including mine, have many pressures on them, the pastor's profession is IMPOSSIBLE to carry out fully and completely!

I found my message for the laymen. This is what I told them:

"If you have a pastor who loves you and can tell you about God's love, thank God for that!

"If you have a pastor who is a 'good' preacher and has any other pastoral talents, thank God and praise Him for His blessings.

"If you have a pastor who is a 'great' preacher, and can administrate, comfort the sick, the grieving, and minister to the general needs of most of the people in the church (and this is by far most of the pastors in our country), Thank God, praising Him, and fall on your knees before Him for having sent you such a man!"[2]

Writing in *Christianity Today*[3] magazine, another author has suggested that we should treat Christian leaders in the same way we would like them to treat us. We can give encouragement and support by:

–believing in them, their potential, their promise, and thanking God for what he has done and is going to do in the church leader's life;

–insisting that the church leader spend times of rest and vacation with the family;

–realizing that he or she may have hundreds of names to remember so we should not get uptight when ours temporarily is forgotten;

–being aware that there are moments when the Christian leader needs to hear the truth spoken in love but without hostility. Such speaking should come because something needs to be said and not because of our own frustrations or anger;

–recognizing that the congregation who hired the church leader did not hire his or her family and therefore should not expect extra work and responsibilities from them;

–honoring the privacy of their personal lives;

–remembering the pressures that are faced by the average church leader. Try, therefore, to be less demanding and more considerate with the pastor and the pastor's family;

–respecting the pastor's personal study time, recognizing that good sermons are not prepared in the midst of constant interruptions;

–periodically telling the church leader that you appreciate his or her work. Such words are much appreciated but sometimes very rare.

Finally, *share the load.* Someone has likened many contemporary churches to a big football game in which a few people, desperately in need of rest, do all the work while thousands of others, desperately in need of exercise, sit on the sidelines watching and sometimes criticizing.

This picture of all the action being done by a few is not a biblical concept. According to the Bible, the church consists of a group of ministers each of whom has gifts to be developed and used for building up the entire body of believers (1 Cor. 12). Only some have special gifts of leadership.

Do you remember how the early church selected lay people who were wise, filled with the Holy Spirit, well respected, and willing to do some of the more routine duties in the church so that the leaders could devote their time to prayer, preaching, and teaching (Acts 6:1–4)? The church leader's responsibility is not to do all the work while everyone else sits back and watches. Instead, the church leader might be what Trueblood[4] has called a "playing coach." He or she is one with special expertise who sometimes "carries the ball" but whose prime task is to encourage, teach, and stimulate other church members in their individual ministries within the body of Christ.

Let us recognize that at no place in the Bible is the pastor elevated to the status of a superstar who does almost everything and who basks in the glory of fame and adulation. No one person can do everything. We who are church members must recognize the pastor's strengths and weaknesses, must resist the tendency to encourage a superstar status for the pastor, must encourage the church leader to share responsibilities, and must take some of those pressures on ourselves. In this way the pastor is freed to develop the priorities of praying, preaching, and teaching, unencumbered by day-to-day activities which could and should be done effectively by trained assistants and lay people.

Caring for Community Leaders

It is easy, perhaps, to care for those Christian leaders whom we know and see on a regular basis, but what about those political leaders whom we may never have met, whom we might not respect, and for whom we may not have voted? The Bible instructs us to show a caring concern for political leaders—a concern, incidentally, which also should be shown to our employers. This caring can be demonstrated by submission, payment of taxes, respecting our leaders, prayer, and involvement in community issues.

Submission. The Bible instructs us to be in submission to the governing authorities. It is God who places political rulers in their positions and he, in his wisdom, "puts down one, and exalts another" in spite of our political preference (Ps. 75:6, 7; Rom. 13:1–3; 1 Pet. 2:13–15).

When Paul instructed believers to obey the government, that government was not very sympathetic to Christians. Thousands had been martyred because of their faith, but the believers, nevertheless, were instructed to submit themselves to the civil authorities as part of their Christian duty.

But what if the authorities gave instruction that contradicted God's teachings? In the Old Testament, Daniel encountered this and concluded, along with the apostles many years later, that when governmental rulings contradict *clear biblical teachings,* the believer must obey God rather than men (Acts 5:29).

In discussing our relationship with employers, we are also instructed to submit to them with all respect and to work with honesty and diligence (1 Pet. 2:18, 19; Eph. 6:5, 7). When he wrote his little epistle to Philemon, the apostle Paul was concerned about a slave named Onesimus. Previously, this man had been useless to his employer but later he became a Christian who ministered to Paul as a friend and brother. Undoubtedly, Paul would have preferred to keep Onesimus but instead the slave was sent back to his master with the promise that Onesimus would now submit to his employer and work diligently. Such is the responsibility of all of us who are employees and who are citizens.

Payment of taxes. Do you remember the time when some of the local religious leaders tried to trap Jesus by asking him whether they should pay tax to Caesar? Jesus asked for a coin and told the people to "render to Caesar the things that are Caesar's; and to God the things that are God's" (Matt. 22:21). On another occasion he instructed Peter to pay the customs tax (Matt. 17:25–27), and in the epistles, we are instructed to pay taxes honestly (Rom. 13:6, 7).

Sometimes, of course, we don't like the way this tax money is spent. We may disagree with our political leaders and at least in some parts of the world we are free to make our disagreements known. But for the Christian, refusing to pay taxes is not one of the options by which we protest what the government is doing.

Honoring our leaders. I once spent several years in the Navy where it was customary to salute senior officers. There were times when some of us resisted because we didn't respect the people in positions of military leadership. "You may not respect the man," we were told, "but respect the position which he holds and salute the position even if you can't salute the individual." If we have difficulty respecting leaders because of their actions, we must nevertheless respect them because God instructs us to do so. That is one of the ways in which we care for political leaders.

Undoubtedly we will need God's help to respect those political leaders who are dishonest, immoral, and concerned with building their own fortunes and prestige. Perhaps, too, we need to remember that God will ultimately judge all people, including those who abuse their authority.

Prayer. Another way to care is to pray with "entreaties and prayers, petitions and thanksgivings . . . for kings and for all who are in authority, in order that we may lead a tranquil and quiet life in all godliness and dignity" (1 Tim. 2:1, 2).

It is, I suspect, difficult to be a political leader, especially a political leader who seeks to be honest, sincere, concerned about one's constituency, and dedicated to doing what is right. United States Senator Mark Hatfield has written about this in one of his books.[5] He describes how difficult it is to avoid the corrupting lust for power that characterizes so many political systems, to avoid feeling pride and self-importance while in office, to resist the pressures of different lobbying groups or blocks of voters, and to stop oneself from lashing out in anger, especially against those people who claim to be Christians but who write letters to politicians that are filled with hatred and condemnation.

To pray for political leaders is good and acceptable in God's sight and one practical way in which we can care for those leaders whom we don't know and perhaps will never meet.

Involvement. Should Christians get involved in political issues? There is nothing in the Bible to suggest that we should withdraw from politics, refrain from voting, or withhold criticism of the government. Jesus himself criticized governmental tyranny when he called Herod a fox (Luke 13:32), and throughout the entire Bible we read examples of godly men and women who both spoke out against political injustice and worked to change social conditions.

Surely God is not pleased with the lackadaisical attitude of many Christians who sit back and do or say nothing about moral corruption, pornography, television violence, persecution of minorities, and other injustices. We serve a God who is in control of all history and as Christians we have a responsibility to speak out and to show how the Word of God applies to the politics of the society in which we live. At times, we will differ as Christians on how we view significant issues. Even when we do agree, we may not be heard, we may be undermined and possibly even persecuted. At such times we should remember the words that Christ gave to his disciples:

> Be on your guard; for they will deliver you up to the courts, and you will be flogged in the synagogues, and you will stand before governors and kings for My sake, as a testimony to them. And the gospel must first be preached to all the nations. And when they arrest you and deliver you up, do not be anxious beforehand about what you are to say, but say whatever is given you in that hour; for it is not you who speak, but it is the Holy Spirit (Mark 13:9–11).

Our task as Christians, according to Senator Hatfield, is to witness to the good news of Jesus Christ "and to build his new society, his Kingdom, which takes root within his Body, the community of believers. Membership in that Body will invariably place the believer in tension with manifestations of earthly power"[6] but our responsibility is still to reach out and do what we can with God's help to change the society in which we live. Even to challenge leaders in the spirit of love is one way to care and help them be more effective in the work which they have been given by God—even though they may not recognize God's hand in their lives.

We often forget about caring for our leaders, but this is commanded in the Bible and surely it must be a concern for every Christian who wants to experience the real joy of caring.

11

Caring about Doubters

HORATIO SPAFFORD WAS a successful lawyer and business-man who lived in Chicago about 100 years ago. He was active in the Y.M.C.A., a Sunday school teacher for his Presbyterian church, and a man who was very much interested in biblical archeology.

Then, in 1871, tragedy struck. The Chicago fire wiped out his real estate holdings along the front of Lake Michigan. Two years later, on the advice of his physician, the family decided to take a vacation in Europe. Spafford sent his family ahead but their ship collided with another vessel in mid-Atlantic and sank. Mrs. Spafford was saved and taken to Wales, but their four daughters all drowned.

When he received the sad cable from his wife, Spafford immediately took a train to New York and was soon on a ship to Wales. As he traveled across the Atlantic he asked the Captain to awaken him when they passed the spot where his four daughters perished. There, on the deck, in the middle of the night, Horatio Spafford wrote the words of a well-known hymn:

> When peace, like a river, attendeth my way,
> When sorrows like sea billows roll;
> Whatever my lot, Thou hast taught me to say,
> It is well, it is well with my soul.

Though Satan should buffet, tho' trials should come,
Let this blest assurance control,
That Christ has regarded my helpless estate,
And hath shed His own blood for my soul.

And, Lord, haste the day when the faith shall be sight,
The clouds be rolled back as a scroll,
The trump shall resound and the Lord shall descend,
"Even so"—it is well with my soul.

Horatio Spafford could have become very bitter—especially after his son died an untimely death in 1880. Spafford could have doubted God's goodness, wallowed in resentment, or seethed with anger. But he continued to trust in God in the midst of tragedy, and this hymn became an inspiration to innumerable people in the century that followed.[1]

Caring about God—and the Problem of Doubt

I have a pretty good idea what some psychologists would say today about Horatio Spafford. They might conclude that he was pretending it was well with his soul. They might argue that he was denying reality and looking for answers in an irrational religion. They would argue that Spafford, and many like him, are deceived in their assumption that God and a devil both exist, that Christ is in control of the universe, and that he is coming again. Many psychologists would agree with Sigmund Freud, the founder of psychoanalysis, who dismissed God as a figment of human imagination and who described religion as a narcotic which we have invented to help us get through the stresses and strains of life.

But Freud's view of God was based primarily on his involvement with neurotic psychiatric patients. His writings give no evidence that he really understood the foundation message of Christianity. Might it be, therefore, that it is the critics who have overlooked the evidence and denied reality? When we consider the orderliness of the universe, the accuracy and profundity of the Bible, the clear intellectual evidence in favor of the Christian message,[2] and the experience of Christians for generations, it probably takes more faith to ignore the facts and not believe, than it does to believe in Jesus Christ and the message of the Scriptures.

If we are going to be caring people, it is important to determine what we think about the universe, whether or not we believe God exists, and how we view the relationship of mankind to any deity.

According to the Scriptures, we human beings were created in God's image and given the freedom to choose whether or not we would obey God. Our forefathers chose to disobey and ever since that time people have been involved in sin. God, however, is holy and cannot tolerate sin or injustice. As a result sinful humans have been condemned to punishment, not because God doesn't like us, but because his holy nature cannot tolerate or overlook our wrongdoing.

But the God who is holy and just is also kind and merciful. He sent his Son, Jesus Christ, to live a sinless life and to die on the cross to take the punishment for our sins. Now, instead of accepting the punishment that is due, we have the privilege of having all our sins pardoned because Christ has already paid the penalty for our wrongdoing.

God has still given us free will, however. Just as he gave our ancestors the freedom to accept or reject him, so today he gives us the freedom to remain in our sins or to invite him into our lives where we allow him to become our Savior and our Lord. To commit ourselves to Jesus Christ and to invite him into our lives is a personal decision that each of us must make for ourselves. When we have the courage to invite Christ into our lives, we have the promise of sins forgiven, of eternal life in heaven with Jesus Christ, and of our whole nature being changed so that we are new creatures, sons and daughters of God himself (1 John 1:9; Rom. 6:23, 8:17; 2 Cor. 5:17; Rom. 5:1).

This is a simple message, but some have never heard it and for this reason have never put their trust in Jesus Christ.

Many of these people are in backward, poorly developed nations; many are in our own country; perhaps some are living next door to us or down the street; and others are faithful members of churches, people who worship regularly and try to live good lives but who nevertheless are not Christians in the sight of God because they have never deliberately committed their lives to Christ's lordship and control.

There are people, however, who have believed and have invited Christ into their lives but are not alive spiritually. Some of these people may not take their beliefs very seriously. Others may be enthusiastic about Christian things but they struggle with periodic doubts concerning the nature of God or the teachings of the Bible.

Regardless of where they are spiritually, surely God is interested in doubters. Surely he wants believers to care for doubters and to show a compassionate concern for each other when we are questioning and struggling with intellectual doubt.

Most of us have heard about "doubting Thomas." He was one of the disciples who was so skeptical that his reputation as a doubter has come down through the centuries. Following the resurrection, Thomas refused to believe that Jesus was alive until more solid proof became available. Later, when Thomas saw Jesus, the Lord did not condemn the doubting. Instead he presented Thomas with all of the evidence needed to persuade a skeptic (John 20:26–29). Convinced by this evidence, Thomas became part of a loyal band of praying believers (Acts 1:12–14), and tradition says that he later became an effective missionary for Christ.

On another occasion, Jesus met a little delegation sent by John the Baptist. John was in prison, perhaps alone and probably in the midst of great discomfort. His messengers wanted to know whether Jesus was really the Messiah or whether they should be looking for someone else. John, you will remember, had introduced Jesus to the world and had preached that he was the Messiah. Surely it must have seemed strange that John, of all people, would begin to question this later in his life. Once again, however, Jesus did not condemn. Instead, he told the delegation to go back and tell John what was happening. Ministries were taking place that could not be done by ordinary men (Matt. 11:1–5). Jesus must have concluded that such evidence would be helpful to a doubter in jail.

Perhaps in these examples we have a guideline for helping those who struggle with doubt. Such people do not need condemnation and criticism. They need understanding and they need someone who will lovingly help them find answers to their questions. To come to the aid of people who struggle with doubts and to help them care about God is one of the most difficult but rewarding ways in which we can experience the joy of caring.

Why Do People Doubt?

We live in an age when people are encouraged to be skeptical. This isn't always bad. Honest doubt and sincere questioning can protect us from error and help us find the truth. For some people, like Thomas, doubt is a temporary condition which stimulates us to find answers and which fades away when the evidence is presented.

For others, however, doubt persists even in the midst of numerous facts and answers. It is difficult enough to care for and to help the doubter who wants answers; it is even more difficult to influence the person who seems unwilling or unable to be convinced regardless of the evidence.

Several years ago in a remote Swiss village, two American missionaries, Francis and Edith Schaeffer, began a ministry which over the years has helped hundreds of people find help with their doubts and answers to their spiritual questions. The missionaries established a center for spiritual seekers and named it *L'Abri,* which is the French word for "the shelter." In the years of its existence, people from all over the world have made their way up the mountain to find this shelter and to seek out those sensitive L'Abri workers whose caring is especially directed toward those who struggle spiritually, intellectually, and psychologically.

One of these workers, Os Guinness, wrote a book recently in which he described some causes of doubt and suggested ways in which we can care for those who struggle spiritually.[3] Guinness maintains that an understanding of doubt helps to protect us against the attacks on our faith and helps to prepare us for the years of testing which Christians may encounter in the years ahead. An understanding of doubt can strengthen our faith especially if we who are believers can openly discuss doubts (as Thomas did) and find support, caring, and answers from other Christians.

According to Guinness there are several causes of doubt. *First, doubt comes when we fail to realize just how much God does for us.* Such doubting is often seen in Christians who become so involved with other believers that they withdraw from non-Christians and fail to appreciate the dramatic contrast which so often exists between those who are followers of Jesus Christ and those who are not. Eventually there is a failure to see a real need for God, and as a result we soon begin to doubt his existence or influence.

When such doubt comes along perhaps there is value in "counting our blessings," pondering what life would be like if we had no belief in God, and developing both a habit of praise and an attitude of gratitude by which we can remind ourselves that God *does* make a difference. Such thinking helps us to turn our backs on self-sufficiency and often doubt gives way to a renewed conviction of God's existence and working.

Second, doubt comes when we have a view of God which fails to appreciate his greatness and, makes him seem too small. If we assume that God is weak, powerless, and not very influential then we begin to wonder if God is really worth trusting. Such thinking, of course, doesn't do anything to change God's nature but it does lead to a mental vagueness which prevents us from believing and trusting fully. This is almost a circular kind of reasoning. We assume that God is not great or powerful so we don't trust him. As a result, we don't see him work and this strengthens our view of the smallness of God. Such doubt needs a clear picture of what God is really like as shown in his Word, the Bible.

Third, some doubt comes because we have never developed solid reasons for believing, and as a result we have no foundation for our faith. Everyone, of course, believes in something. To live meaningful lives each of us must make some assumptions about the universe; otherwise our lives would be characterized by chaos. But what do we believe, and why do we believe?

Many people never ask this question. They're not sure what they believe, they have no solid reasons for the beliefs they do have, and since there is "no reason why" they should believe, there really is "no reason why not." Without a solid foundation based on factual evidence, their faith is shaky and easily swayed.

God, who created our minds, is not threatened or weakened by the serious questions which come from inquiring individuals. It is a healthy exercise periodically to write down what we believe and why we believe as we do. If we don't know what we believe and can't find answers, then we can get help from discussions with a caring, thinking friend and from reading books which help us to find answers to our questions.[4]

A fourth cause of doubt comes because we are involved in religion but have never made a solid personal commitment to Jesus Christ. We live at a time when a variety of beliefs are tolerated and when few people take their faith seriously. Many grow up in the church and take in their parents' religion without giving the issue much further thought. Others latch onto religious systems that are sensational, that make no real demands, or that currently are popular.

What happens to these people when problems come along? What happens when their religious beliefs are challenged? How does their faith hold up when they are forced to suffer? At such times the beliefs of many people crumble because their faith is built on personal convenience or popular fads, not on sincere commitment. Guinness writes that "the idea of a healthy faith that has no personal commitment is a contradiction in terms."[5]

During the Second World War an Austrian psychiatrist by the name of Viktor Frankl spent several years in a Nazi prisoner of war camp. As he watched his fellow prisoners, Frankl realized that the prisoners who survived were those who believed in something with conviction. People who had half-hearted beliefs sometimes would wither and die, not so much because of the physical suffering but because they had lost all purpose for living.[6]

Do you believe anything so much that you are willing to commit your whole being and your life, if necessary, to your cause? If not, perhaps now is the time to examine your beliefs. As Christians we ask Christ into our lives by a personal individual act of commitment. We grow through Bible study and the supportive encouragement of one another. But when we face death or persecution often we are forced back on our own again. Each of us must stand or fall alone. Whether we stand or fall depends on the personal convictions that we develop now, while persecution is not very prevalent.

Some people, however, become believers but fail to mature. They remain what Paul called spiritual babies. Perhaps they know about theology but they rarely put their faith into practice. This brings us to *the fifth cause of doubt—doubt which comes because people cease to use their faith.*

Do you know people who once were enthusiastic Christians but who no longer seem to have much interest in spiritual things? It may not be that these people have lost their enthusiasm because of the intellectual arguments of some skeptic. More likely, such people have simply drifted away. They have become busy with other things, have left their first love, and eventually have discarded their faith not because it was useless and didn't work, but because it was simply unused.

Faith is like a muscle which must be used if it is to get

stronger but which wastes away if it is never exercised. Faith is a relationship with another person which either grows when we spend time and energy to make it grow or drifts off into unimportance when we become busy with other things.

Do you remember the church at Laodicea, described in Revelation 3:14–18? They had begun enthusiastically, but in time they had become so involved with other things that their faith became lukewarm. As a result there was no longer a dynamic relationship with God. Instead there was a cooling of interest which surely was one step removed from slipping into doubt.

The sixth cause of doubt comes when we have let our emotions take over so that we are not thinking clearly. Emotions, of course, are an important part of our being and they do much to make our lives exciting and meaningful. But emotions can be very influential, especially when we are bursting with happiness or, in contrast, when we feel discouraged, rejected, or guilty. At such times it is easy to question the truth and reality of our intellectual beliefs.

When emotions take over, they cause our thinking to waver and sometimes we reach faulty conclusions about life. Have you ever noticed, for example, how we can be shaken by criticism? In response to critics it is so easy to conclude that we really *are* incompetent and this can plunge us into discouragement and self-condemnation. At such times consciously and deliberately we must rethink what we know to be true about ourselves and our abilities. In like manner, we periodically must review the reasons for our beliefs. Reason and emotion are both important in life, but decisions, especially decisions about our faith and our future direction in life, must be built not on what we *feel* to be true but on what we *know* to be true.

According to Os Guinness, *the last cause of doubt is that which comes from a fear of what might happen if we dare to believe.* Here is an unwillingness to believe because we are afraid of being hurt, of being disillusioned, of being ridiculed, of making a mistake, of losing our friends, of having to change our life style, or possibly of being persecuted.

In Chapter 1, we considered a fear of love. Now we see that there can also be a fear of belief. Just as we must risk giving ourselves to others if we are to experience human love, so we must risk committing ourselves to the Lordship of Jesus Christ if we are to experience a sense of conviction, unhampered by this kind of doubt.

Caring about Those Who Doubt

It is not easy to care for a doubter. It can be time-consuming, intellectually challenging, and sometimes very threatening to discover that another human being rejects the message which we believe is not only important, but which has implications for eternity. And what if we are not sure in our own beliefs? Then we feel uncomfortable when another person raises questions which we cannot answer.

Let's recognize at the beginning that we rarely help people if we tell them to "stop doubting" or to "simply believe." These are things which cannot always be done at will. Also, it doesn't help much if we preach little sermons (assuming vainly that this will dissolve another's inner struggles), if we ignore the doubter, if we react in anger, or if we stifle the doubter's questions.

Far more important for the doubter is someone who is willing to listen with compassion, acceptance, and love even though in listening we may hear ideas that distress us and questions which we are unable to answer. Listening with compassion is the first step in caring for a doubter.

The second step involves trying to determine if the doubter really wants answers. Sometimes it is more comfortable or more convenient to doubt than to believe. At times people use doubt as an excuse for complaining or for not getting involved with others. In some cases, expressions of doubt become like a club by which a young person, for example, can challenge an older person or by which a spouse can "needle" his or her mate. People who doubt and don't want to face the evidence are not likely to be persuaded by arguments or by hearing reasons for belief. It is more effective to pray for them and to display acceptance and love.

If we can assume that the doubter seriously wants to find answers, however, then we reach a third step in helping. We try to determine what is causing the doubt and then guide the seeker in a search for answers. Probably no doubter will change without considering at least some evidence. Like Jesus with Thomas and with John the Baptist, we must attempt to understand the doubter and present evidence to meet the needs of the one seeking a reason to believe.

But what if we don't have the evidence? What if the doubter's questions leave us confused? In such situations, if we are unable to help we should say so, recognizing both that it takes time to think through answers and that doubts sometimes disappear very slowly. There can be value in seeking further information from books or from some better informed believer. In our search, we can recognize that God does not leave us to flounder forever. He will provide answers and reassurance in due time, or he will give us a willingness to trust him even if we do not understand.

And what if no satisfactory answers are found and the seeker's doubt disintegrates to disbelief? What if our counseling fails to help and the other person's problems go from bad to worse?

In such situations it is easy to condemn ourselves and to conclude that we are failures. Since we all make mistakes, sometimes, of course, the fault is ours. Some of our mistakes can have serious consequences. Remember, however, that even God, who is sovereign and all powerful, does not always see events turn out as he surely wants. He can make anything happen but he loved us enough to let his children have the freedom even to rebel against him. He let the rich young ruler hear the message but turn away, and he saw Thomas doubt repeatedly in spite of all the evidence. For reasons which we humans do not always comprehend, some people are never helped, never persuaded to put their trust in Christ, never free from their doubts. This can be painful and deeply disappointing to those of us who want to care, but our task is to still go on caring and trying to help.

We may never have all of the answers, but like Horatio Spafford, we also can rest in the knowledge that if we know God, and his characteristics, that we can go on living meaningful lives, even though we do not always understand his ways and timing.

Part III
The Practice of Caring

12

Caring and Feelings

JOAN WINMILL BROWN is an actress.

Born in England and raised in somewhat unstable circumstances, she became a secretary but soon was attracted by the lure of the theatre. She joined several traveling theatrical companies, appeared in the West End (the Broadway of London), spent time with the great actresses and actors in England, and developed close friendships with several well-known people. Life for this talented young actress was filled with accolades and praise, but it was also empty.

"There was a constant fear of loneliness," she wrote later. "Deep down inside I was afraid of the future, afraid of being alone, even though I had many friends; John (the man whom she was dating) basically had the same fears. Perhaps our greatest fear was of being failures in life. I believe so many people are drawn together in this way and that is why there are so many unhappy relationships. For it is not based on real, giving love, but purely on a need to be loved."[1]

Life in the theatre was draining, and the young actress experienced first one emotional collapse and then another. She described the experience in vivid language:

For weeks I had sensed a feeling of desperation and a longing for peace. It seemed as if the struggle to try to make

145

a career was futile, for my health would so often keep me from attending auditions. . . . My confidence was gone. I dreaded getting out of bed in the morning and having to face people. The thought of even crossing a street would send fear running through me.

What was happening to me? In the past I had always been game to try anything. I had enjoyed the unexpected telephone call that sent me racing out of the apartment, bound for some delightful discovery. Now, I dreaded to hear the phone ring. . . .

I looked at myself in the mirror and saw a person who looked old beyond her years. No amount of makeup could hide the lost expression in my eyes. Someone has said that the eyes are "the windows of your soul." These "windows" were misted over with the effect of so many drugs— prescribed of course, but nevertheless eating away any spontaneity that might still be left. They were red-rimmed from crying. I despised my weakness and, in so doing, despised everything about myself.

Every day I would read in the paper of people who were far worse off than I—people starving, people bereaved. Many times I had wanted to be able to reach out and perhaps help, but always this *me* seemed to get in the way. My life seemed so utterly useless.[2]

Later in the darkness of a lonely apartment, this lady recognized how meaningless life had become:

My career as an actress had spanned eight years. It had included roles in a number of films, in addition to many stage parts and television appearances. Yet my life at twenty-seven was, putting it mildly, a mess. My health was broken. I could not work properly, and nothing seemed worthwhile. Apart from the complexity of my life, I knew I was on the verge of a third breakdown. Life held nothing for me. That morning I had read of an actress friend who had committed suicide. I envied her. *How* I envied her! Her battles were over; mine were still going on, and I didn't have the energy or desire to strive anymore.[3]

Then someone invited this actress to a Billy Graham Crusade meeting in London. She went to laugh and to please her friends, but she came away changed, a woman whose life had been transformed by Christ who came in, took control, and for the first time brought real peace and stability.

This was the beginning of a new life but it was not the end of problems. Suffering and pain come to the children of God as well as to nonbelievers, and Joan Winmill Brown, like the rest of us, has had struggles in her Christian life and periods of discouragement. But her commitment to Christ has enabled her to handle these emotions and to experience the caring that comes from others who have stuck with her and helped her through times of stress.

Hurting—Alone and with Others

Everyone has feelings. At times we all feel lonely, angry, discouraged, or embarrassed.

Such feelings can be frightening. A sense of helplessness, intense love, an upsurge of anger, excitement, overwhelming depression, fear, or a need for other people, can all be so threatening that we often pretend such emotions don't exist. We may smile with an outward show of tranquillity while inside we struggle to avoid those situations and people that could arouse any feelings which might just get out of control.

But God gave us feelings: emotions to be experienced and expressed rather than stifled. Of course, he created us as thinking people and people whose lives consist of actions. But our feelings influence our thinking and how we act, just as our thoughts determine how we feel or what we do, and our actions influence how we feel and how we think.

At times we all suffer and feel the intense physical and psychological pain which, even if it lasts for only a short time, can serve as a warning that something is wrong inside.

But what if that pain persists? What if we don't get better? What about people who spend their lives in wheelchairs or in hospital wards? What about the people with birth defects or a persistent mental illness? How do these people handle their suffering? How do we feel about this and how do we help?

It is difficult for any of us, no matter how empathic or sympathetic, to stand in a healthy body and sense the real pain experienced by another who is hurting. In an earlier chapter we mentioned the three men who came to help Job but who criticized, argued, and preached instead. These "helpers" seemed oblivious to the physical pain and intellectual struggle that were tearing Job apart. Little wonder that he became angry! The fourth helper, Elihu, was more understanding, and it was he who helped Job to rise victorious over his woeful condition.

People react in different ways when they are hurting. Some deny that they hurt, attempt to push their pain aside, pretend it isn't there, stifle questions of "why," and ignore any feelings of anger or bitterness. Others honestly acknowledge their hurts but suffer alone. They may develop an attitude which says "nobody will ever understand who hasn't been through something like this." As a result, silent suffering leads to the building of psychological barriers which keep other people out. Then come feelings of self-pity, hopelessness, and a poor self-image. Others could help with these attitudes, but in our age of rugged individualism many persons resist such help and attempt to "go it alone." This isn't easy but sometimes suffering in silence is easier and less risky than trusting others with the details of one's deepest needs.

Frequently, as they suffer alone, people try to find ways to help themselves. By a process of trial and error, mixed with the results of past experiences, such persons often are able to deal successfully with the problems of life—at least for a while. At times they turn to the literally hundreds of self-help books which recently have flooded the marketplace offering psychological, medical, and spiritual advice on a wide range of human problems. In addition, there are tapes, seminars, radio broadcasts, magazine articles, sermons, and public lectures, all of which have been useful to some hurting people, especially those who are reluctant to admit to others that they have a need or could benefit from being helped.

But suffering alone can also be self-defeating. Without

the objectivity, support, and encouragement of others who care, there is a tendency to withdraw into our own little worlds of self-pity, helplessness, and bitterness. The Bible, as well as common sense, tells us that suffering must be shared. The sufferer and those who care must bear one another's burdens (Gal. 6:2) in times of need.

There are both healthy and unhealthy ways of doing this. The hurting person, for example, can suffer with others in an irresponsible manipulative way. Complaining, moaning about one's fate, making others feel guilty because *they* are not hurting or doing enough, placing excessive demands on one's friends, or expecting people to do what can be done by oneself—all of this can lead to a helpless self-pitying attitude. This is little different from the attitude of those who suffer alone—except for the fact that others have been pulled into the sufferer's misery. By shifting blame and responsibility onto others, the sufferer has found a way to avoid facing and doing something about his or her own problems.

An honest sharing of feelings or hurts and a respect for the needs and schedules of others is much healthier. It must be coupled with a willingness to let others help. When we accept help in a time of need, we show respect to others and give them the privilege of ministering to us. Allowing others to care for us sometimes is one of the best ways in which we care for others.

It is not easy to receive help, just as it is not easy to give help. Sometimes when we are in need and people reach out to help, we may lack the energy to communicate our needs and to accept the care when it is given. At such times the helper may not know what to do. Our theological beliefs may seem threatened in the face of unexplainable suffering, and it may seem easier to withdraw where we can suffer alone. But in both the receiving and the giving of help God expects us to care for one another. It is important, therefore, that each of us has a willingness to show helpful behavior when we can, and to accept the help of others when we need it and when it is offered. To accept this help may be especially important when we are lonely, when we are anxious, and when we are discouraged.[4] In the remainder of this chapter we will discuss each of these common emotions.

Loneliness

Loneliness has been called the most devastating sickness of this age—a problem that plagues more people than any other. It is a painful, unwelcome feeling of frustration, helplessness, and loss of contact with others. Unlike solitude which is a refreshing time away by ourselves, loneliness is unwelcome and sometimes agonizing.

The causes of loneliness are complex. Sometimes it comes because we have been cut off from other people—as the grieving person who has lost a loved one, the teenager who has been criticized by adults or rejected by his peers, the married person who is ignored by a spouse who is too busy with things outside or around the home, or old people whose friends have died and who feel there is no place for them in the society.

Sometimes loneliness comes because we push other people away by our uncooperative attitudes or by critical, sarcastic, unloving comments. People who have strong inferiority feelings often conclude that no one would want to spend time with them so they stick to themselves, refuse to get close to other people, and then wonder why they sense a desperate loneliness. This loneliness, incidentally, further convinces them that they are not liked, and this increases their feelings of inferiority.

Our mobile society also creates loneliness. In the United States alone it is estimated that one-quarter of the entire population moves every year. People, therefore, are less inclined and less able to develop lasting friendships. In addition, there are those in positions of leadership who sometimes are lonely because they know that it is neither a wise nor good use of time to build intimate relationships with people who are "under" them.

Although loneliness often arises because of these separations from other people, we should also recognize that people are lonely when they are cut off from God. He created us to have fellowship with him, but when mankind rebelled against the Creator, we cut ourselves off from this closeness. When we are separated from divine companion-ship we are incomplete. This often results in a restless loneliness.

It follows, therefore, that one of the first and most important ways of dealing with loneliness is to come back to God through faith in Jesus Christ. When we confess our sins and tell God that we believe in his Son, Jesus Christ, then we belong to him. His Holy Spirit lives within us and we have communion with God so that we are no longer alone.

In the Garden of Eden, however, Adam knew God well, but the Creator nevertheless stated that people also need human companionship (Ge. 2:18–25). To deal with loneli-ness we need other people. We don't sit around feeling sorry for ourselves, hoping that someone will come to us. Instead, we need to ask, "How can I be involved with others?" Then, with God's help, we must reach out—to greet one another, to serve one another, to be devoted to one another. This does not mean that friendships will arise spontaneously and loneliness will disappear automatically. For loneliness to decline we must work to get along with people, determine to communicate, and do what we can to remove any attitudes which might alienate us from others. Then we must spend time in the presence of other people even though we may not always feel like it.

Do you remember how we began this book—with my account of those lonely days in London several years ago? I didn't solve the loneliness by sitting in my room hoping that someone would come and meet my need. I began talking to others and doing things for them. Before long my loneliness had evaporated. Whether we seek to escape or avoid loneliness, we need to reach up to God for fellowship with him and reach out to one another in loving acts of kindness and service. These are among the most rewarding ways to experience the joy of caring.

Anxiety

Anxiety is a feeling of threat, apprehension, and uneasiness. In a mild form, anxiety, like any other emotion, can be good. It alerts us to possible danger and prepares us for action. When anxiety builds, however, it can dull our thinking, bring about discouragement, take the joy out of life, and often produce a number of physical symptoms such as stomach upsets, headaches, and pain all over the body. In its extreme form, anxiety produces a reaction similar to panic which immobilizes a person and tenses the entire body.

Most psychologists would agree that anxiety is different from fear. Fear is an emotional response which comes when we consciously recognize that there is a real threat, danger, or problem. Anxiety, by contrast, is a feeling of apprehension which does not stem from any reasonable cause that we can identify. Some psychologists suggest it comes because of unconscious conflicts, guilt which we don't face, hostility which we deny, insecurity because of past problems, or our having expectations for ourselves which we can never succeed in attaining.

Worry is closely associated with anxiety, and often we use the two words together. Worry involves fretting over real or imagined problems. Most of us recognize that the things we worry about almost never happen, but that doesn't stop us from worrying. When such worry consumes our thinking we are hindered from effectively dealing with the problem. H. Norman Wright, a licensed marriage counselor and psychology professor, has made some very interesting suggestions for dealing with worry and anxiety. These are presented in Table 2.

But how do we care for someone who is anxious and filled with worry? Let us recognize from the beginning that it does not help to tell the person to "stop worrying." That is easier said than done and implies that worry can be turned off voluntarily and automatically.

Table 2
How to Deal with Worry and Anxiety

1. Be sure you have had a complete physical by your physician. Have him check glands, vitamin deficiencies, allergies, exercise schedule, and fatigue.
2. Be aware of all of your emotions. Face your worries. Don't run from them for they will return to haunt you. Admit that you do worry or have anxiety (but only if you really do). Do not worry about worrying. That just reinforces and perpetuates the problem.
3. Write down the worries and anxieties that you have on a piece of paper. Be very specific and complete as you describe them.
4. Write down the reason or cause for your worry. Investigate the source. Is there any possibility that you can eliminate the source or cause for your worry? Have you tried? What have you tried specifically?
5. Write down how much time you spend each day worrying.
6. What has your worry accomplished in your life? Describe in detail. Describe the benefits of worrying.
7. Make a list of the following:
   (a) How many times has my worrying prevented a situation from occurring?
   (b) In what way did my worry increase the problem?
8. If you are nervous or jumpy, try to eliminate any sources of irritation. Stay away from situations that increase this until you learn how to react differently. Try to remove the source of irritation. For example, if the troubled world situation gets to you, why listen to so many newscasts? What do you do to try to relax? Can you read, work in the garden, ride a bike for several miles? Avoid rushing yourself. If you worry about being late, plan to arrive at a destination early. Give yourself more time.
9. Avoid any type of fatigue—physical, emotional, or intellectual. When a person is fatigued, difficulties can loom out of proportion.
10. When you do get involved in worry is it over something that really pertains to you and your life or does it properly belong to someone else? Remember that often our fears or worries may be disguised forms of the fear of what others think of us!
11. When a problem arises, face it and make a decision as to what you can do about it. Make a list of all of the possible solutions and decide which you think is the best one. If these are minor decisions, make your decision fairly quickly, taking more time for major ones. A person who is a worrier usually says, "I can't decide. I go over and over these problems and cannot decide which is best." Look at the facts and then decide, but do not continue to worry about it. After you have looked at the facts and made your decision, do not question your choice. Otherwise the worrying pattern erupts all over again. Do not begin to debate your own decision. Practice this new pattern of making decisions. If you do fail in the beginning, do not give up. Your old pattern has been locked in because of long use, and you need to practice the new pattern of thinking for a while before it begins to work successfully. As soon as possible act upon your decision and get rid of the problem.

It is interesting to notice, however, that the Bible seems to say just that. In Philippians 4:6, 7 we are told not to worry or be anxious about anything, but (and this is what makes the biblical comments practical) we have some guidelines on how to do this—guidelines that we might use in caring for others who worry. The worrier is told first to place his or her confidence in God, rejoicing in him. Second, one must always remember that the Lord is near even in times of difficulty. Third, we can "tell God every detail of your needs in earnest and thankful prayer" and expect that the peace of God "which transcends human understanding, will keep constant guard over your hearts and minds as they rest in Christ Jesus" (Phil. 4:6, 7, Phillips). Then, finally, we should let our minds think on the things that are holy, right, pure, beautiful, and good.

To stop worrying is not to let our minds go blank. That will only last for a while and then the worry comes back. According to the Bible we must replace the worrying by prayer and a trust in God. Often we can help one another to keep this perspective in times when it is much easier to slip into a destructive attitude of anxiety.

Hans Selye,[5] a well-known and widely respected expert on the problem of human stress, has challenged the common conclusion that ours is a special age of anxiety. Most of the stresses that once bothered people, he maintains, simply have been replaced by new stresses. Nevertheless, Selye does believe that there is one stress problem which is particularly unique in our time. It is the problem of not having a philosophy of life or a system of belief which can motivate us and guide our behavior. Undoubtedly Selye is correct in his conclusion that much anxiety comes because people have nothing in which to believe—even though Selye himself has a non-Christian approach to life.

In contrast the Christian casts all of his or her worries and anxieties on God (1 Pet. 5:7) believing that he cares for us, will strengthen us, and will guide us in times of difficulty. We can also be assured that he will give us peace.

Biblical peace is not a mood of blah indifference, smug

self-complacency, or unruffled serenity. Christians, like non-Christians, will continue to have anxieties and concerns about life's circumstances, but the peace from God assures us that no matter what happens we have a deep-down certainty that a loving sovereign God is clearly in control and will, in the end, make everything work out for our good. We can care for anxious people by sticking with them in times of pressure, by letting them know of our interest, by praying for them regularly, and by reminding them of the peace of God which Jesus gives (John 14:27) and which sustains us especially in times of anxiety and worry.

Discouragement

It is easy to become discouraged, to feel pessimistic, apathetic, unhappy, self-condemning, helpless, and inclined to give up on life. Massive quantities of research have been done on this common human emotion and innumerable books and articles have been written both to help the discouraged and to instruct counselors on the treatment of depression.

Depression often comes because of physical reasons—poor sleeping and eating habits, chemical imbalance, physical infections, or the influence of drugs. When a person is depressed, especially for long periods of time (several weeks or months), he or she should be encouraged to see a physician so any physical causes of depression can be treated. If the depression still persists, it is important that a qualified professional counselor be consulted. Often depression has complex psychological causes best handled by counselors who have special training. Referring needy people for professional help is one of the most effective ways in which we can care for others.

Nevertheless, it is valuable to recognize that depression sometimes happens when we have become angry and try to hide the fact (anger will be dealt with in the next chapter). At other times we become depressed because we have lost a loved one, a job, or some important opportunity (losses will be discussed in Chapter 14). But depression also can come when we slip into negative thinking.

Have you ever noticed how our emotions frequently are affected by our thinking? It is almost impossible, by an act of will, to stop feeling depressed. But if we work to change our thinking then the feelings of depression often disappear automatically.

Several years ago an interesting theory was proposed by a psychologist named Albert Ellis.[6] The theory assumes, first, that our emotions are caused by and controlled by thinking. When we think something is tragic, we feel sadness. When we think something is dangerous, we feel afraid. When we think something is wonderful, we feel excited. It follows, therefore, that the way to change or control our feelings is to change and control our thoughts. But how is this done?

According to Ellis, we human beings keep talking to ourselves all the time. We don't usually talk out loud, of course, but we carry on a communication with ourselves during most of our waking hours. Much of what we tell ourselves is irrational, unrealistic, and self-defeating. We tell ourselves, for example, that we are incompetent, that we are unlikely to succeed, that people don't like us, that we are likely to fail, and so on. Ellis has suggested that to change a person we must change his or her thinking so that one thinks thoughts which are more rational and less self-defeating.

When a person is depressed there is value (either alone or with the help of a friend) in looking at what one is thinking. Then we should ask some questions: Is the thought really accurate? What proof do we have that it's accurate? Is the situation being interpreted correctly? Could there be some other explanation? Perhaps more than anything else, depressed persons need to get a realistic perspective on life, and this can often come from a caring friend who dares to challenge the depressed person's thinking and conclusions.

This doesn't always work, however. Often when we become depressed we seem to enjoy it for some reason—at least for a while. In feeling sorry for ourselves and thinking that everyone else is against us, we can wallow in our misery. For most of us, however, this doesn't satisfy for very long. We need, therefore, to recognize that our own thinking may be creating the problem and then we need to get a more realistic perspective on our situation.

Do you remember Elijah? He was an ancient prophet whom God dramatically used to condemn all the heathen prophets of his time. But when Queen Jezebel decided to murder the prophet, he fled to the wilderness, begged God to take away his life, and apparently was overwhelmed by depression.

Then an angel of the Lord came to Elijah and first dealt with his physical need. Elijah was given food, drink, and a chance to rest. Second, he was given the opportunity to express his feeling and to get the problems "off his chest." Then, third, the angel challenged Elijah's thinking, showed him that he was not alone or in danger of death (which was what he had convinced himself of), and taught him how to think differently. Before long Elijah was back in contact with other people and free from his depression.

Perhaps that angel is a good picture of how we can care for others in times of depression—encouraging them to get physical help, urging them to express their feelings, and helping them to think more clearly.

Emotions are powerful, but they add zest to our lives. They are not something to be feared, but they must be controlled and channeled. Helping one another, especially in times of loneliness, anxiety, and discouragement can be a significant way for us to experience the emotion of joy which comes from caring.

13
Caring and Self-control

SHORTLY AFTER HIS graduation with a degree in counseling, one of my students wrote a letter to describe his first few months on the staff of a psychiatric clinic. He described some of the joys and difficulties in counseling but then went on to report that the most surprising thing about his new job was the number of patients who appeared to be seething with anger. "Sometimes, the people realize that they are angry and are unwilling or unable to do anything about it," this former student reported. At other times, however, the patient cannot see that anger, bitterness, and an unwillingness to forgive have become ingrained at the core of life. Other people might see this, but the angry person does not.

Anger, of course, is very common. At times it wells up in all of us, causing thoughts and actions that we may regret later. If we are going to care for people we must learn to help them with their anger, and we must recognize that our own caring can be blocked by the anger within ourselves.

Caring and Anger

Anger is a strong feeling of tension and aggressiveness which arises when we feel threatened, frustrated, or wronged. It is an emotion which churns up the entire body, produces abundant energy, and at time spills out in physical violence or, more commonly, in verbal aggression, such as critical comments or cutting sarcasm. Some professionals would agree that unacknowledged or unresolved anger is at the basis of most psychiatric problems.[1] It can destroy us physically, psychologically, and spiritually. And certainly it does not disappear just because one becomes a Christian.

Anger can be harmful. When we become angry our blood pressure increases, the heart beats faster, more adrenalin goes into the blood stream, our muscles tense up, and our digestive processes stop. If the anger persists, the body remains ready for action and eventually begins to break down physically. Little wonder that high blood pressure, heart attacks, strokes, digestive problems, and muscular aches and pains often occur in people who remain in heightened and prolonged states of anger.

Even as anger can be harmful physically, it can also harm us psychologically. When we are angry we have difficulty making rational decisions. We don't think logically and sometimes jump to conclusions which intensify our anger but which are not based on factual evidence. It is a widely held psychological principle that when anger is held within it often leads to depression—a conclusion which is acknowledged in the Bible where fathers are told not to provoke their children to anger lest they become discouraged (Col. 3:21).

In addition, anger often creates barriers between people. If we attack or criticize others in our anger, this in turn cuts us off from others and leads to loneliness. It has been suggested that the loneliest person of all is the one who is angry.

Anger is not always wrong. It should not be assumed that anger is always harmful or always sinful. We know that God is angry at times (Ps. 7:11) and that Jesus became angry during his time on earth (Mark 3:5). To say that anger is always wrong would be to imply that Jesus "lost his cool" periodically and slipped into sinful behavior. This, of course, is inconsistent with the biblical teachings about Christ's holiness. Apparently, therefore, there are different kinds of anger: that which is harmful and that which is not harmful.

There are several different words in the Greek language which have been translated "anger" in the English New Testament. The first of these is the Greek word *orge*. This was the term used to describe the anger of Jesus when he drove the money changers out of the temple (Mark 3:5), and it is the word used in Ephesians 4:26 where we read "be angry, and yet do not sin." *Orge* anger is an intense but righteous indignation over sin and wrongdoing in the world. According to one writer[2] such anger is *without malice or resentment;* directed not at the wrong done to oneself but at injustice done to others; controlled, rather than heated and unrestrained; directed against wrong deeds or unjust situations rather than against people; and geared not only to criticism but to positive and constructive action which will eliminate wrongs and bring about change for the better. It is very easy, however, for righteous *orge* anger to burn within us and to lead us into a sinful vindictive lashing out.

The second Greek word for anger is *parogismis* which means a bitter irritation and exasperation. This is the word translated anger at the end of Ephesians 4:26. When we let it persist, even overnight, the devil uses it to get a foothold in our lives (Eph. 4:27). This in turn creates the harm that we described earlier in the chapter.

The third word for anger is *thumos* used in verse 31 of Ephesians 4. It refers to a boiling agitation or an outburst of intensely hostile feeling which, along with bitterness and slander, should also be put out of our lives.

Unhealthy anger can be controlled. Of course it is not easy to eliminate anger from our lives. Sometimes we like being angry, and without always being aware of it anger lets us experience a sense of power and superiority while we dwell on the things which make us mad. Most of us, however, don't enjoy being angry. We would like to take action to control the anger in our own lives and to help others who are struggling with the problem of uncontrolled anger.

To control this emotion, we first must face the fact that

we are angry, and then express our feelings. Following a talk on anger, I once was approached by a lady who had never realized that Jesus became angry. She expressed amazement that a Christian should openly admit his or her wrath. "I thought we weren't ever supposed to be angry," she said, "and for many years, whenever I've felt angry, I have tried to pretend that the anger wasn't there." When anger is denied and hidden like this we really are burying a problem. The buried anger then is likely to come out in resentment, psychological problems, or physical reactions such as were described earlier. When we feel anger it is best that we honestly face up to these feelings and express them.

Anger, then, can be expressed in ways that are destructive or in ways that are good. Harmful expression comes when we explode quickly, in hot temper (Prov. 4:29, 15:18) and with yelling of harsh words or violence. This, of course, lets us express the way we feel, but it pushes other people away, causes them to be angry in return, and afterward leads us to feel guilty and sometimes anxious. Explosive anger, therefore, can be more harmful than helpful.

It is much better to stop ourselves before expressing how we feel. (There is value in the old system of counting to ten before we say anything.) Perhaps this is what the biblical writers had in mind when they told us to be slow to anger or to restrain our angry words (Prov. 16:32; 19:11; James 1:19). Then, in a calmer manner, we can express our feelings to God and to the persons involved. Comments such as "This whole situation is really making me angry" or "I really was aggravated by your comment" express our feelings without hurting and alienating others.

I was once told that it is good never to raise one's voice. While that isn't always easy, anger which is expressed without raising one's voice is anger which can be dealt with effectively, and resolved without hurting people or raising tension.

The second way to deal with anger is to redirect it. Instead of brooding or "boiling in hostility," there can be value in taking a walk, working in the garden, playing a game of tennis, or doing anything else which gives us the opportunity to express and release pent-up energy. This is of special help when we cannot do anything to change the circumstances which are making us angry in the first place.

In addition, there can be value in thinking about our anger rationally. Is the situation that made us angry really worth all the emotion it is arousing? Is there a way in which our anger could be channeled into some kind of activity that would solve the problem which made us angry? Are we hanging on to a sinful attitude of anger because we are enjoying it when really we should be committing it to God and asking him to remove it? When we look at the facts do we have good solid reasons for being as angry as we are? Some people try to answer these questions on paper (which is another way of expressing our feelings) and some might prefer to talk them over with a caring friend. If you are that friend, it might be helpful to share some of the above principles with the person who is angry.

But what do we do when people explode at us in anger? Several years ago I used to drive a small Volkswagen which collided, one day, with a big Lincoln Continental. To put it mildly, the other driver was livid with anger. He called me names, in front of the gathering crowd of spectators, and proclaimed that I was at fault and a menace to the motoring public. I'm sure I felt anger, aggression, and frustration in return, but rather than exploding I calmly offered to call the police and to do what I could to help him continue on his way as soon as possible. The man was so surprised at my response that within half an hour he apparently had forgotten the scratch on his fender and even offered to drive me wherever I wanted to go—while the tow truck picked up the scattered front portion of my little car. Having watched this from the crowd an acquaintance later reminded me of Proverbs 15:1. Harsh words stir up anger, we read, but "a gentle answer turns away wrath."

Surely it is no accident that the discussion of anger in Ephesians 4 ends with instructions to be kind to one another, tender-hearted and forgiving each other, just as

God in Christ has forgiven us (Eph. 4:32). Perhaps, after acknowledging, expressing, and reevaluating our anger, we need to replace our angry thoughts with kind actions and a willingness to forgive.

Caring and Forgiveness

Forgiveness is a theme that runs throughout the pages of the Bible. When we confess our sins to Jesus Christ, we are promised that he will forgive (1 John 1:9). Then, in the Lord's prayer, we are instructed to forgive others just as Christ forgave us (Matt. 6:12).

To forgive is to pardon completely and to forget the offense forever, without holding a grudge and without maintaining an attitude of condescending superiority because of what we have done.

There are times when every human being loses control. We explode in anger, say things that should not have been said, gossip, harbor jealousy or envy, think sexual thoughts which shouldn't be there, engage in sexual acts that are neither honoring to God nor beneficial to us, or otherwise give in to subtle temptations. Sometimes we admit these tendencies, at least to ourselves, and recognize the presence of guilt because of our thoughts or actions. At other times we pretend to "have it all together" and walk about like the Pharisees of old claiming to be something that we are not.

When we lose control it is important to remember that all of us are sinners, but because Christ died on the cross and paid for our sins, everything is forgiven—past, present, and future (1 John 1:7–10). Whenever we lose control or slip into sin we can confess directly to God and know for certain that he will forgive without requiring that we do anything to atone for our wrongdoing.

At times, however, there can be value in confessing not only to God but to our fellow human beings. One way to care for others is to confess to one another, pray for one another, forgive one another, and accept each other with all of our human imperfections (James 5:16; Eph. 4:32; Rom.

15:7). Since God is clearly willing to forgive, we have a responsibility to do the same.

But isn't it easier to hold a grudge? At times, doesn't it feel more satisfying to give in to bitterness? Isn't it difficult, perhaps impossible, to really forgive completely? Surely true forgiveness is possible only when God's Holy Spirit, who dwells within us, gives us the power to reach out to those who have wronged us and to forgive unconditionally. When we refuse to do this, we are ignoring what the Bible has commanded us to do. We are harboring an attitude which is self-destructive and which undermines our relationship with God and with others (Heb. 12:14).

In addition to forgiving others we also must be willing to forgive ourselves. Since God forgives us what right have we to wallow in self-condemnation because of our past actions? Many people know intellectually that they are forgiven but they don't feel forgiven. As a result they continue living in self-condemnation and unhappiness. Do you remember the man who came to Jesus and said, "Lord, I believe, please help my unbelief?" When we have difficulty forgiving ourselves, perhaps we, like that man, should pray, "Lord, thank you for forgiving me. Help me now to forgive myself."

As Christians, therefore, we are to recognize that God forgives, that we are to forgive others, and that we must forgive ourselves. But there is one other aspect of forgiveness which for some people is very difficult. At times, we must *accept* forgiveness.

Several years ago the chaplain at a large mental hospital made an interesting comment to some friends over coffee. "The problem with many of my patients," he said, "is that they cannot accept forgiveness." The major step in accepting forgiveness is to remind ourselves that God forgives us. This is stated clearly in the Bible (1 John 1:9), and we can ask God to help us really accept this forgiveness. In addition, it often helps when other people care enough to show that they forgive too.

Joan Winmill Brown has told about visiting a jail in

Honolulu where she met a girl who had grown up in a Christian home and knew much about the Bible. "There's no hope for me," the girl lamented. "I've known about God but I have failed him so terribly. There's nothing anyone can do."

Mrs. Brown reached for her Bible and read 1 John 1:9. "If we confess our sins, He is faithful and righteous to forgive us our sins and to cleanse us from all unrighteousness."

The girl resisted. "I know that verse. That won't help me!"

But Mrs. Brown continued, "Don't you see God is saying he will forgive *all* unrighteousness?"

The girl looked at the words on the page and suddenly her face lit up. She had never seen the little word "all." For the first time she realized that God would forgive *everything* she ever had done wrong. As she prayed that Christ would forgive everything and control her life she was flooded for the first time with this startling realization—there really was hope for her!

From that point on the girl's life changed dramatically not only because she recognized that God forgives, but because with his help and with the help of a friend she was able to reach out and accept that forgiveness. In the months that followed she continued as a prisoner. But she knew that when the Son of God makes you free you are really free (John 8:36) even when in jail or imprisoned by difficult circumstances. In sharing these biblical truths, Joan Winmill Brown had reached out to care for someone who needed to experience and accept forgiveness.[3]

Caring and Pressure

Have you ever noticed that some of our biggest problems in life come when we are under pressure? Our work, our studies, community projects, family responsibilities, social obligations, the things which must be done at church—these and a host of other demands have made this an era when thousands of people struggle to cope with the stresses and pressures of life.[4]

Sometimes, but not always, pressures can lead to anger, faulty thinking, guilt, interpersonal tensions, impatience, loss of self-control, and an unwillingness to accept forgiveness. When these emotions are combined with the pressures of life it becomes extremely difficult to get along efficiently and we become prime candidates for emotional and physical breakdowns.

For a long time I worked on the assumption that to be under pressure was a sign of weakness. People were pressured because they had not organized their time properly. As a result they were reaping the fruits of their own inefficiency. At times, that does happen but there are other times when pressures come because of circumstances over which we have no control.

Not long ago this happened to me. Due to circumstances, mostly beyond my control, I found myself swamped with extremely pressing demands in my work. My wife began to wonder whether I would be able to handle the load. It didn't help that I had once written a book on stress because that made we want all the more to handle the pressure efficiently and without showing signs of weakness.

During those hectic days I learned some lessons which might apply to anyone who faces pressure. I learned again that when pressures build up the body often grows weary so we are in special need of proper sleep, exercise, recreation, and "time off." When we're under pressure we're inclined to forget these things and to push ourselves almost beyond endurance.

I also learned the value of talking it over with two or three caring friends who listened, encouraged, and tried to take off some of the load. They helped me keep a perspective on my life and work, challenged me when I began to get angry or started to see things from a narrow perspective, and helped me to think of ways in which I could cut back on the workload.

In addition, I began to ask myself, "What will happen if I don't get everything done?" To be honest, I had to answer that life would go on, that the world would not collapse, that the cause of Christ would still advance, and that I would probably be a lot healthier. I developed a new attitude which said, "I'll do what I can as best I can. I will not try to do everything or always to do things perfectly." With this perspective I was able to continue with my work—less pressured, more relaxed, and with greater efficiency.

Perhaps one of the most meaningful ways by which we can experience the joy of caring is to help each other recognize the harmful effects of excessive pressure and change our attitudes toward the demands on our time and energies. In so doing, we can help each other control and handle the pressures of life.

14

Caring and the Future

NOT LONG AGO my wife and I were standing in the foyer of church chatting informally with some friends following the morning service. As we talked we were joined by an acquaintance whose first words were unexpected:

"I filed for divorce yesterday!" she said. She then went on to describe some of the problems she and her husband had had in the months previously. We talked about her children and how they were reacting. She shared her loneliness, her sense of failure, and her concern that people would now reject her because the marriage had been a failure.

"I have been crying for days," she continued, "but somehow I've got to pick up, go on, and provide a stable home for the children."

During our lengthy conversation my mind went back to another lady, a television talk-show hostess who had invited me to be a guest on her program. During a series of breaks for commercials she told me about the pain of divorce and her struggle in terminating a marriage.

There are thousands of people like these women and their husbands who have lost a loved one through separation or divorce. Such people grieve like those who lose loved ones through death, through the breakup of a romance, or through the separation which comes when moving tears us away from family and significant friends. Leaving home, changing jobs, moving or seeing others move, watching our children go off to college, retiring—these are among the losses that each of us experiences as we go through life. Each of these brings pain and a sense of grief. Each stirs up feelings of emptiness, loneliness, sadness, and sometimes fear. At such times we may not feel like eating. We may be unusually tired, sense little hope for the future, and have a lack of energy. On occasion there is shock, anger, depression, denial that the loss is taking place, and a long period of struggle before we can accept the inevitable. In all of it there is a need for other people to help fill the void. Such caring people don't always replace the lost love, but they do show that we are still appreciated, understood, and cared for.

My friend on the television talk show told me about a little book which had helped her to survive the loss of a love.[1] The authors give advice which surely is comforting and reassuring. They have suggested, for example, that people who experience a loss need to:

–Expect to feel shock and emotional numbness as you struggle to accept the reality of the loss.

–Admit that it hurts and that the hurt is normal if you are to ever heal.

–Recognize that others have encountered similar painful experiences and that most people survive and heal in time.

–Acknowledge that healing is slow, like "a lightning bolt, full of ups and downs, progressions and regressions, dramatic leaps and depressing backslides." Sundays, weekends, and holidays are the worst times.

–Get a lot of rest, try to stick to a regular schedule, and eat a proper diet.

–If possible, don't make any major decisions at least immediately. Beware of the rebound, the tendency to fill up the loss too quickly by rushing prematurely into new romantic attachments.

–Accept the fact that it's okay to get support, understanding, and comfort from other people.

–Don't isolate yourself from life or try to hide from the reality of a situation.

–Make an agreement with a friend, someone whom you can call and talk with whenever things get tough.

–Accept the fact that you may feel depressed, angry, lonely, and vulnerable.

–Beware of addictive activities like alcohol, drugs, eating, or television.

–Keep a journal of your thoughts and emotions so that these ideas can be expressed on paper. Later it will be possible to look back to see how healing has taken place.

–Learn to forgive, to start anew, to invite new people into your life, to develop new interests, and to reach out to do something for someone else.

–Reaffirm your religious beliefs and your faith in God.

As we go through life most of us will experience losses of people, of jobs, of positions, of youth, and sometimes of stability. All of these are difficult; all are better dealt with when there are people around who are willing to understand and care. This is especially true when we lose our health or when we face the pain of death.

Caring and Sickness

As everyone knows, sickness involves discomfort, pain, and inconvenience. It comes, at times, without warning and is a reminder that we are human beings with physical, emotional, and spiritual limitations. Sickness drains our energy, forces us to withdraw (temporarily or permanently) from our ordinary activities, and makes us feel helpless. It can also make us feel angry, guilty, and afraid. When sickness leads to hospitalization we can experience a separation from loved ones, a loss of privacy, a removal from familiar surroundings, and the need to rely on the help of strangers. When we are ill we cannot always control our activities, our appearance, and our destinies. We are forced to be dependent on other people and sometimes must live with a gnawing uncertainty of not knowing why we are sick, whether we will get better or when. It is little wonder that people like to ignore symptoms and deny the reality of sickness. Little wonder that they struggle with questions like "Why me?", "What will become of me?", or "What will I do now?" Some people express these frustrations by withdrawing from others, refusing to accept help, grumbling in bitterness, or using their illness (or sometimes their assumed illness) to manipulate others.

When we are ill it is difficult to see how anything positive might come from the experience. Nevertheless, from his perspective in dealing with hundreds of sick and terminally ill patients, a chaplain named Vernon Bittner reached some interesting conclusions about the value of illness:

> As a parish pastor I was convinced that illness could be one of the most important opportunities a person could have. During that time I saw numerous people use their experience of illness to mature as persons, to grow in wisdom, and to serve others. For them illness was not a waste of time, but an encounter with a part of life they had not met before. Through their illness they had discovered how their Christian faith was related to the prevention and cure of illness. Their faith not only provided help to accept illness, but also revealed spiritual and emotional benefits from their illness. . . .
>
> I know how difficult it is to use illness constructively, whether a person believes in God or not. I also know that the experience of illness often becomes the opportunity many people need to stop running long enough to find a happier, more fruitful life. Sometimes a person does have to get sick to get better, at least emotionally and spiritually, if not physically.
>
> The more I am with people who are sick, the more I realize how difficult it is to face illness. . . . Illness, like nothing else, makes us aware of our own limitations. This can encourage us to be more open to ourselves, others, and God, or it can result in our being more closed as individuals. . . . Unfortunately, too many people look at illness as a waste of time or as something to be avoided. They do not see it as an opportunity for maturity, wisdom, and service.[2]

Chaplain Bittner went on to describe how his own illness taught him more fully to see the love and forgiveness of God. The sickness changed him from following a path of self-destruction to "a new life of being alive to God, to others, and to myself."

But not all patients or their families are able to benefit from sickness. It is especially difficult to let ourselves grow when an illness is terminal or when we are faced with the prospect of a life with permanent disability. Even when we experience something no more serious than the "24-hour flu" it is easy to be annoyed about our sickness. We try to maintain our independence and stubbornly refuse to let other people help, to let them experience the joy of caring.

To care for another person at a time of sickness can involve such obvious practical activities as giving physical care, financial help, or babysitting and meals for the family. But caring also means being available to spend time with someone who wants to talk, listening to expressions of anger and discouragement, and leaving when the sick person really wants to be alone. To care is to be friendly, cheerful, and encouraging without being unrealistically optimistic or insensitive to the sick person's troubles. To care is to promise to pray for the patient during the illness and to follow up this promise with action. At times we may want to share something from the Bible and at other times we may want to sit in silence and "just be there." When we care we let people verbalize their fears and feelings and to the best of our ability we help them find answers to the "why?" questions.

In all of this it is difficult not to learn some things about ourselves, to thank God for our own health, and to realize with the apostle James that "you do not know what your life will be like tomorrow. You are just a vapor that appears for a little while and then vanishes away" (James 4:14).

But life does not vanish away forever, even when illness gives way to death. Life on earth is only a prelude to life in eternity—and for the Christian our experiences on earth teach us patience and prepare us for heaven where there is no sickness and no death.

Caring and Death

Several years ago a Chicago psychiatrist named Elisabeth Kubler-Ross published a book describing her involvement with terminally ill patients.[3] When people are approaching death, she observed, they often go through five distinct stages.

The first stage is one of *denial* in which the patient and his or her family have difficulty accepting the fact that the illness is terminal. None of us wants to believe that death may be near, and to handle the shock people try to deny the truth of the diagnosis.

Before long such denial gives way to a second stage—that of *anger:* "Why did it happen to me?" "Why doesn't God do something?" "Why couldn't it have been somebody else?" These are the kinds of questions which, if not expressed verbally, may lurk in the patient's mind and sometimes lead to an irrational, but understandable, lashing out at other people.

The third stage is *bargaining,* trying to make a deal with God. It's the kind of reaction Hezekiah had in the Old Testament when, faced with death, he attempted to bargain with God for a longer life.

The fourth stage is one of *depression.* As the illness lingers on it is easy to become discouraged, especially if one's physical condition gets worse and there is an anticipating kind of grief at the thought of coming death and separation.

Acceptance is the final stage when the patient begins to withdraw from other people and appears more and more willing to accept the imminent departure from life.

These five stages may not be seen in everyone, especially if the length of illness is short. Also, the five stages often overlap so that they don't always occur in order. And throughout all of this most people maintain at least some hope. According to Kubler-Ross, when a patient stops hoping this usually is a sign that death is near.

David Hubbard recently watched his mother face her own death and concluded that God knows about these stages.

He understands our emotions as we face death in ourselves or in a loved one and undoubtedly he goes through the stages with us since there is no experience that touches us without touching him.[4]

This does not mean, however, that death holds no fear or that Christians always face it with an attitude of calm indifference. The Bible describes death as an enemy. By his death and resurrection, Jesus conquered death and some day will raise all believers to a better life. Until then death is a sting which hurts.

Corrie ten Boom, whom we mentioned earlier, saw many people die during her lifetime, but one of her first experiences with death came when she went as a child, with her mother, to visit a family who had lost a young baby. She described her reactions many years later:

> It was strange that a society which hid the facts of sex from children made no effort to shield them from death. I stood staring at the tiny unmoving form with my heart thudding strangely against my ribs. Nollie (Corrie's sister) . . . stretched out her hand and touched the ivory-white sheet. I longed to do it too, but hung back, afraid. For a while curiosity and terror struggled in me. At last I put one finger on the small curled hand.
>
> It was cold. . . .
>
> That night as he (Corrie's father) stepped through the door I burst into tears. "I need you!" I sobbed. "You can't die! You can't!"
>
> Beside me on the bed Nollie sat up. "We went to see Mrs. Hoog," she explained. "Corrie didn't eat her supper or anything."
>
> Father sat down on the edge of the narrow bed. "Corrie," he began gently, "when you and I go to Amsterdam—when do I give you your ticket?"
>
> I sniffed a few times, considering this.
>
> "Why, just before we get on the train."
>
> "Exactly. And our wise Father in heaven knows when we're going to need things, too. Don't run out ahead of Him, Corrie. When the time comes that some of us will have to die, you will just look into your heart and find the strength you need—just in time."[5]

Corrie found that strength many years later when she was taken into the cold, impersonal prison hospital to look into the face of her sister who had died in the concentration camp.

> I raised my eyes to Betsie's face. "Lord Jesus—what have You done! Oh Lord, what are You saying! What are You giving me!"
> For there lay Betsie, her eyes closed as if in sleep, her face full and young. The care lines, the grief lines, the deep hollows of hunger and disease were simply gone. In front of me was the Betsie of Haarlem, happy and at peace. Stronger! Freer! This was the Betsie of heaven, bursting with joy and health. Even her hair was graciously in place as if an angel had ministered to her.[6]

Recently we received a letter from a gracious lady who had lost her husband after a short and unexpected illness. He had been a committed Christian who discussed death openly with his family during the days before he died and who rested confident in the knowledge that for the Christian to be absent from the body is to be present with the Lord.

Almost a year after he died his wife wrote, "I won't try to pretend that it has been easy. I have felt lost and lonely, confused and uncertain. I don't begin to understand God's dealings with us but I take each day, often each hour, a step at a time. He gives us strength and courage to endure and to wait for Him to show me the next step. I know in my head and my heart that God is in control and doesn't make mistakes, but I have to rely on Him even for the faith to trust Him. He knows me and what I can stand so I trust Him to supply what I need. Life isn't as much fun without my husband—much of the sparkle is gone—but we look to Him to keep His promise to turn our sorrow into joy and help us to honor and glorify Him in this most difficult experience."

Grieving almost always begins with a period of shock, even when we were expecting the death. Usually there is great sadness, physical symptoms such as insomnia or stomach upsets, periods of despair, and often futility. Questions of "why?" and "what will we do now?" persist, especially as the mourner attempts to pick up life again and move on.

At such times there is a great need for support from others. There is a need to express sorrow and sometimes anger, and the need to accept the reality of a loss. At times the grieving person wants to talk; at other times he or she prefers silence but usually with the knowledge that there is someone nearby who cares and is concerned. Special days—like Christmas, the dead person's birthday, or anniversaries—can be especially difficult, and at such times small gestures of kindness and remembrance are appreciated deeply.

Although there are similarities in how we respond to death, it is important to remember that no two people die alike, and neither do any of us grieve alike. But Christians have a like hope for the future. Since Jesus died and rose again, we who are believers expect someday to rise as well, to meet him, to see our loved ones again, and to be with the Lord forever. Little wonder that the Scriptures tell us to "comfort one another with these words" (1 Thess. 4:13–18).

Caring and Life

When we think about the certainty of death surely we must ponder life and how we are living it. In a hundred years most of us will have died. What kind of life will you have lived?

Someone has said that if you want to find out what we really consider important in life we should look into our checkbooks to see how we spend our money—and look at our calendars to see how we spend our time. It might also be good to look into our minds to see what we think about, especially during those unguarded reflective moments when we are not occupied with the business of day-to-day living.

Our life styles, including how we spend our money, how we spend our time, and how we think, can give a good indication of how we are spending our lives and what we consider important. Some people drift through life with no particular goals except to get along from day to day. Others go through life with very specific goals, often geared toward the acquisition of wealth, status, or security. It is important for each of us to decide, periodically, what is really important in life, to decide on some goals for the future, and to ponder how we would prefer to spend the days that remain between now and that uncertain time when we will die. Such a reevaluation enables us to live lives that are more meaningful, more satisfying, and very often more caring.

It is important, first, to *decide on our goals.* Sometime soon you might ask yourself the following questions and write your answers on paper: What are my lifetime goals? How do I plan to spend the next five years? How would I live if I knew that in six months I would be dead? What do I really think God wants me to be doing with my life? If such questions bring forth lists of goals, aspirations, and priorities, put a number one beside the most important, write a number two beside that which is of second importance, and continue down the list. Then we should think of some specific practical ways by which we can work to attain these goals. Without such deliberate goal-setting we are inclined to drift through life and never achieve what we would like to accomplish.

Second, it is important to *organize our time.* A widely repeated story describes how the president of a large steel company once contacted a management consultant and asked, "How can I get more things done? If you can show me a way which works I'll pay anything within reason."

The consultant gave a concise reply. "Take a piece of paper," he said, "and write down the things you have to do tomorrow. Then, number the items in their order of real importance. Start in the morning working on number one until it is completed, then go to number two until that is completed, and keep on going until the end of the day. If you can't complete everything don't worry, but repeat this procedure every day."

A few weeks later the management consultant received a

check for $25,000 from the grateful company president who said that this lesson was the most valuable one he had ever learned in his business career. By stopping at the end of one day to consider what needs to be done the next day, we are able to move ahead efficiently and productively.

I am convinced that God never gives us too much to do. We may take on too much, we may fall into the habit of compulsive overwork, we may waste our time so that our lives are marked by inefficiency and lack of productivity, but God gives each of us 24 hours in a day and is willing to help us accomplish his goals for our lives during that time period.

Third, we can *avoid the "tyranny of the urgent."* I think it was Charles Hummel who first used this term to describe the common habit of always doing what is most pressing and never having time to accomplish long-range goals.

Jesus very easily could have fallen into this way of living. People were around him making demands all the time but he still seemed to get things done. Perhaps this was because he had a habit of getting up early in the morning, withdrawing to a solitary place, and asking the Heavenly Father to give him a clear perspective on the day ahead (Mark 1:29–35). It is true, of course, that he never had to deal with telephones, junk mail, traffic jams, and electrical appliances that don't work. But he did have to deal with inefficient people, traveling on foot, and the pressure of crowds, some of whom were critical, demanding, and inconsistent in their attitudes. Little wonder that he needed to manage his time well, to get rest whenever he could, to spend time in prayer and worship, and to withdraw periodically to visit with his friends.

This leads us to a fourth way to live a life which is productive and meaningful: *hang loose.* It is important to recognize that things can go wrong—friends drop in, needy people phone us at times, we get sick on occasion, unexpected delays and interruptions are a part of life. We need to remind ourselves that "ten years from now our present frustrations won't make much difference," to realize that

God knows even about the frustrations, and to push along doing the best job we can in spite of the interruptions. Remember that God, and your really close friends, value you for who you are and for what you are becoming; not for what you have accomplished. To go through life with a more relaxed attitude enables us to live longer, healthier, more productive lives than we would have if life was characterized by rigidity and an inability to adapt to changing circumstances. To a large extent hanging loose depends on our attitude and mind-set. Our friends can help us to keep things in perspective and so can our God when we let him communicate to us daily through the Word of God.

When we have clear goals, time that is organized, freedom from the tyranny of the urgent, and an ability to hang loose, we are more open to the needs of people around us and more able to relax and to know the joy of caring.

Epilogue

IN A CREATIVE attempt to promote a book, one of my publishers once designed a bumper sticker which read "Be a People Helper." The bumper sticker was a bright yellow and blue, easily attached to the rear of the car. For some reason, however, I preferred to keep my bumper sticker in a drawer. Jokingly, I explained that it might be embarrassing to be driving home some night, to see some poor motorist with a flat tire at the side of the road, but to hurry on by, close enough for him to read my "Be a People Helper" bumper sticker.

At times I have to ask myself if I really want to be a people helper. Do I really want to care? Caring for people takes time. Often it is inconvenient and tiring. Sometimes we are criticized for caring, and there are times when we will be manipulated, taken advantage of, and not appreciated. Commitment to anything worthwhile is costly and that includes the commitment to care for others.

Perhaps one of the reasons why we resist caring is that it interferes with the self-centered drive for success which characterizes so much of our contemporary style of life. Most of us want to be successful in life, and the drive for success does not always leave time for the inconvenience of caring.

In the Old Testament, Joshua was a man called to lead the Israelites into the Promised Land after Moses died. The

180

responsibility must have been great, and Joshua could have been insecure about his responsibilities. So God gave him some advice about success.

"This book of the law shall not depart from your mouth, but you shall meditate on it day and night, so that you may be careful to do according to all that is written in it; for then you will make your way prosperous, and then you will have success" (Josh. 1:8). The secret of success, Joshua was told, was to meditate on the Word of God, to become familiar with it, and then to carefully obey God's Word.

In the New Testament there is an equally powerful directive. Jesus had pointed out that within the world great men were those who had status and authority, but he told the disciples, "It is not so among you. . . . Whoever wishes to become great among you shall be your servant, and whoever wishes to be first among you shall be your slave" (Matt. 20:26, 27). In the eyes of Jesus, success and greatness come to those who are willing to serve. Even as he finished his teaching, two blind men appeared who interrupted Jesus as he walked to Jericho. These people so touched him with their need for healing that Jesus was "moved with compassion" and reached out to give them their sight (Matt. 20:29–34).

Could this be a formula for successful living: meditating on the Bible, observing God's Word, and seeking to be servants? As Christians we do not have the privilege of deciding whether or not we will care. Obedience, love, and caring are the primary marks of a disciple of Jesus Christ (John 13:34, 35). We no longer offer the sacrifices that were part of Old Testament Judaism. Jesus Christ, who died on the cross, has paid for our sins so the shedding of blood is no longer necessary. But the kind of sacrifice God wants today is verbal praise, thanksgiving, and behavior which involves "doing good and sharing" (Heb. 13:15, 16). It is true that caring will involve inconvenience at times, but to reach out in Christian love to fellow human beings is personally rewarding and Christ-honoring. It is the mark of a truly successful individual, and it is a way in which we can experience lasting joy—the joy that comes from caring.

Notes

Chapter 1

1. Material in this section and in portions of chapter 2 is taken from Milton Mayeroff, *On Caring* (New York: Harper & Row [Perennial Publishers], 1971).
2. Ibid., pp. 8, 9.
3. F. Riessman, "The 'Helper-Therapy" Principle," *Social Work*, 10 (1965): 27–32.
4. A. Gartner and F. Riessman, *Self-Help in the Human Services* (San Francisco: Jossey-Bass, 1977).
5. Quoted in J. Allen Thompson, "Gather the Harvest with Joy," *Harvest Today*, 33:3–5.
6. J. Dwight Pentecost, *The Joy of Living* (Grand Rapids: Zondervan, 1973), p. 19.

Chapter 2

1. C. B. Truax, "Therapist Empathy, Genuineness, and Warmth and Patient Therapeutic Outcome," *Journal of Consulting Psychology*, 30 (1966): 395–401.
2. Material in this section is adapted from Milton Mayeroff, *On Caring* (New York: Harper & Row [Perennial Publishers], 1971); and Chester Custer, *Called to Care* (Nashville: Tidings, 1974).
3. Gordon W. Allport, *The Individual and His Religion* (New York: MacMillan, 1950).
4. Marshall Bryant Hodge, *Your Fear of Love* (Garden City, N.Y.: Doubleday [Dolphin Books], 1967).
5. Ibid., pp. 144–45.
6. Ibid., pp. 186-88.
7. W. Schofield, *Psychotherapy: The Purchase of Friendship* (Englewood Cliffs, N.J.: Prentice-Hall, 1964).

8. E. Stotland, *Psychology of Hope* (San Francisco: Jossey-Bass, 1969).

Chapter 3

1. L. Sanny, "Discipling: The Navigators Mission I," *Navlog* (April 1978): pp. 13, 14.
2. L. Sanny, "Discipling: The Navigators Mission II," *Navlog* (July 1978): pp. 12, 13.
3. Ibid., p. 13.
4. For an elaboration of these principles and the basis of Covenant Groups, see Louis H. Evans, Jr., *Creative Love: Covenant Groups . . . How Christians can help each other through loving, caring, sharing and praying together.* (Old Tappan, N.J.: Revell, 1977). Chart reprinted with permission of Louis H. Evans, Jr.
5. The following paragraphs are adapted from Chester Y. Custer, "The Profile of a Caring Church," *Called to Care* (Nashville: Tidings, 1974), pp. 53–55.

Chapter 4

1. The life story of Joni Eareckson is told in her book *Joni* [by Joni Eareckson with Joe Musser (Grand Rapids: Zondervan, 1976)] and in a full-length motion picture, *Joni,* produced by World Wide Pictures.
2. Quoted in Phillip Yancey, *Where Is God When It Hurts?* (Grand Rapids: Zondervan, 1977), p. 113.
3. C. S. Lewis, *The Problem of Pain* (New York: Macmillan, 1962).
4. C. S. Lewis, *A Grief Observed* (New York: Bantam Books, 1961), pp. 4–5.
5. C. S. Lewis, *The Problem of Pain,* pp. 33–34.
6. John White, *The Cost of Commitment* (Downers Grove: InterVarsity Press, 1976).

Chapter 5

1. M. Kelsey, *Healing and Christianity* (New York: Harper & Row, 1973), p. 114.
2. For a summary of current Christian approaches to counseling see Gary R. Collins, ed., *Helping People Grow* (Santa Ana, Cal: Vision House, 1980).
3. C. B. Truax and K. M. Mitchell, "Research on certain therapist interpersonal skills in relation to process and outcome," in A. E. Bergin and S. L. Garfield, ed., *Handbook of Psychotherapy and Behavior Change: An empirical analysis* (New York: Wiley, 1971), pp. 299–344.
4. J. D. Frank, "The Medical Power of Faith," *Human Nature,* 1 (August 1978): 40–47.
5. See, for example, Gary R. Collins, *How to be a People Helper* (Santa

Ana, Cal.: Vision House, 1976); and Paul Welter, *How to Help a Friend* (Wheaton, Ill: Tyndale, 1977).
6. See, for example, Walter McQuade and Ann Aikmann, *Stress* (New York: Dutton, 1974).
7. The author has written a book on stress and how it can be handled effectively. See Gary R. Collins, *You Can Profit from Stress* (Santa Ana, Cal.: Vision House, 1977).
8. Gary R. Collins, *Effective Counseling* (Carol Stream, Ill: Creation House, 1972), p. 20.
9. This is the title of an excellent book by Myron Augsburger. *Caring Enough to Confront* (Glendale, Cal.: Regal Books, 1973).
10. W. E. Hulme, *Dialogue in Despair: Pastoral commentary on the Book of Job* (Nashville: Abingdon, 1968), pp. 128–29, 134.

Chapter 6

1. Paul Tournier, *The Strong and the Weak* (Philadelphia: Westminster, 1963), pp. 18, 20–21.
2. John D. Carter, "Maturity: Psychological and Biblical," *Journal of Psychology and Theology,* 2 (Spring 1974) 89–96.
3. This sentence is based on Genesis 1:27; Romans 3:23; 2 Corinthians 5:17; 1 Corinthians 12:14–25.
4. Elton Trueblood, *A Place to Stand* (New York: Harper & Row, 1969), p. 60.
5. W. Ross Foley, *You Can Win Over Weariness* (Glendale, Cal.: Regal Books, 1978), pp. 55–58.

Chapter 7

1. Material in this chapter is adapted from the author's book (now out of print), *Living in Peace* (Wheaton: Key, 1970).
2. Dietrich Bonhoeffer, *Life Together* (London: SCM Press, 1954), pp. 13–14.
3. John W. Drakeford, *People to People Therapy* (New York: Harper & Row, 1978), p. 98.
4. Francis Schaeffer, *How Should We Then Live* (Old Tappan, N.J.: Revell, 1976), pp. 205, 250.

Chapter 8

1. Gene A. Getz, *The Measure of a Family* (Glendale, Cal.: Regal, 1976), pp. 12, 13, 20.
2. This covenant is reprinted and discussed in a book by the author. See Gary R. Collins, *Family Talk* (Santa Ana, Cal.: Vision House, 1978).

Chapter 9

1. Sherwood Eliot Wirt, *The Social Conscience of the Evangelical* (New York: Harper & Row, 1968), p. 3.

2. For a further discussion of these issues see the books by David O. Moberg, *Inasmuch: Christian Social Responsibility in the Twentieth Century* (Grand Rapids: Eerdmans, 1965); and *The Great Reversal: Evangelism versus Social Concern* (Philadelphia: Lippincott, 1972).
3. Lois M. Ottaway, "Read, Baby, Read: A First Step to Action," *Christianity Today*, 14 (Dec. 19, 1969): 16–18. Portions of this chapter are adapted from the last chapter of a book edited by the author: Gary R. Collins, ed., *Our Society in Turmoil* (Carol Stream, Ill.: Creation House, 1970).
4. Garrett Hardins, "The Tragedy of the Commons," *Science*, 162 (1968): 1243–48.
5. Bibb Latane and John M. Darley, *The Unresponsive Bystander—Why Doesn't He Help?* (New York: Appleton-Century-Crofts, 1970).
6. Warren A. Jones, "The A-B-C Method of Crisis Management," *Mental Hygiene*, 52 (January 1968): 87.

Chapter 10

1. D. Stuart Briscoe, "So You Want to Go into the Ministry, Do You?" Commencement address delivered to the graduating class of Trinity Evangelical Divinity School, June 9, 1978.
2. Quoted by Lucille Lavender, *They Cry, Too! What You Always Wanted to Know about Your Minister But Didn't Know Whom to Ask* (New York: Hawthorn, 1976), pp. 61–63.
3. This section is adapted from Cliff Stabler, "The Care and Feeding of Shepherds," *Christianity Today* (April 27, 1973): pp. 14, 15.
4. Elton Trueblood, *The Incendiary Fellowship* (New York: Harper & Row, 1967), p. 43.
5. Mark O. Hatfield, *Between a Rock and a Hard Place* (Waco: Word, 1976).
6. Ibid., pp. 73–74.

Chapter 11

1. Adapted from Charles Johnson, *One Hundred and One Most Loved Hymns* (Delavan, Wis.: Chas. Hallberg, 1976).
2. For further discussions of these issues, see Clark H. Pinnock, *Set Forth Your Case: An Examination of Christianity's Credentials* (Chicago: Moody Press, 1967).
3. Os Guinness, *In Two Minds* (Downers Grove, Ill.: InterVarsity, 1976).
4. Three excellent books dealing with Christian beliefs are Paul Little's *Know Why You Believe* (Downers Grove, Ill.: InterVarsity, 1967); John R. W. Stott's *Basic Christianity* (Downers Grove, Ill.: InterVarsity, 1958); and C. S. Lewis' *Mere Christianity* (London: Fontana Books, 1952). See also the book by Pinnock (footnote 2 in this chapter).
5. Guinness, op. cit., p. 124.

6. V. Frankl, *Man's Search for Meaning* (New York: Washington Square Press, 1959).

Chapter 12

1. Joan Winmill Brown, *No Longer Alone* (Old Tappan, N.J.: Fleming H. Revell, 1975), pp. 52–53. Ms. Brown appears in a film on her own life, *No Longer Alone,* produced by World Wide Pictures.
2. Ibid., p. 57–58.
3. Ibid., p. 10.
4. It is, of course, impossible to deal with these emotions in a few pages. Interested readers may want to read books by Vernon Grounds, *Emotional Problems and the Gospel* (Grand Rapids: Zondervan, 1976); H. Norman Wright, *The Christian Use of Emotional Power* (Old Tappan, N.J.: Fleming H. Revell, 1974); and Gary R. Collins, *Overcoming Anxiety* (Santa Ana, Cal.: Vision House, 1973).
5. Hans Selye, "On the Real Benefits of Eustress," *Psychology Today,* 11 (March 1978): pp. 60–64, 69–70.
6. Albert Ellis, "Rational-Emotive Therapy," in Leonard Hersher, *Four Psychotherapies* (New York: Appleton-Century-Crofts, 1970), pp. 47–83.

Chapter 13

1. Albert Rothenberg, "Distinguishing the Character and Functions of Anger," *Roche Report: Frontiers of Psychiatry* (World Wide Medical Press) 2, no. 7 (April 1, 1972): p. 5.
2. H. Norman Wright, *The Christian Use of Emotional Power* (Old Tappan, N.J.: Revell, 1974), pp. 112–116.
3. Joan Winmill Brown, *No Longer Alone* (Old Tappan, N.J.: Revell, 1975), pp. 154–55.
4. Gary R. Collins, *You Can Profit from Stress* (Santa Ana, Cal.: Vision House, 1977).

Chapter 14

1. Melba Colgrove, Harold H. Bloomfield, and Peter McWilliam, *How to Survive the Loss of a Love* (New York: Bantam, 1976).
2. Vernon J. Bittner, *Make Your Illness Count* (Minneapolis: Augsburg, 1976), pp. 11, 12, 13.
3. Elisabeth Kubler-Ross, *On Death and Dying* (New York: Macmillan, 1969).
4. David Allan Hubbard, *Why Do I Have to Die?* (Glendale, Cal.: Regal Books, 1978).
5. Corrie ten Boom, with John and Elizabeth Sherrill, *The Hiding Place* (Minneapolis: World Wide Pictures, 1971), pp. 50, 51.
6. Ibid., pp. 216–17.

Questions for Further Thought and Discussion

Prepared by Lawrence M. Tornquist

The value of a book can be greatly increased when readers pause to think about the ideas that have been presented, and when these ideas are discussed with others. The following questions are designed both to stimulate personal thinking or group discussion, and to help readers as they become more involved in acts of caring.

The questions may be discussed by as few as two people, or by a larger group. For best results it is recommended that you do not let your group become larger than 8–10 persons, that you meet on a regular basis (perhaps weekly), that all participants be encouraged (but not forced) to discuss, and that the group members attempt to encourage and stimulate each other to be more caring persons. Take your discussions seriously but don't be afraid to laugh and to experience the joy that comes both from caring and from meeting with others in a small group.

Chapter 1

1. In this chapter the author asks the question: Does Jesus care? Christians often hear much about how God cares when we are hurting and about how he will meet our needs. How have you experienced the care of God when you were hurting?

2. The author suggests that there are risks involved when we care. What kind of risks have you encountered in your caring? How could you prepare yourself for the possible risks involved in caring?

3. In this chapter the "Helper-Therapy-Principle" was discussed. What is this principle? Do you agree or disagree with this principle? Give your reasons. How has caring benefited you? How does this principle relate to the "joy" aspect of caring discussed at the conclusion of this chapter?

4. At one time or another probably all of us have experienced the inability to accept care from others. How have you attempted to push people away when they have offered their care and concern? What were your reactions to others when they refused to accept your care? What would be a good way to handle the refusal of your caring?

Chapter 2

1. The author lists a number of traits which characterize caring persons. Remember it is a rare individual who possesses all of these. What caring traits are present in your life and what ones are not? Of the traits which need development, pick one and describe how you will begin to develop this trait.

2. Openness and honesty are included among the characteristics of a caring person. Why are these important in the caring person? What possible dangers do you see in being open and honest with people? How can you avoid these dangers?

3. Self-acceptance also is listed as a characteristic of caring persons. What do you accept about yourself? What is difficult for you to understand and accept about yourself? Be specific. What are some possible ways in which you could gain deeper self-awareness and greater self-acceptance?

4. Why do you want to care for people? List your reasons. The chapter indicates that our reasons for caring sometimes are selfish. Do you have selfish motives for caring? How are you going to deal with the motives you would like to change?

Chapter 3

1. It is suggested in this chapter that instead of being critical of the church, we should get involved. What have been your attitudes toward the church? In what ways have you been involved? How can you be more caring in your church?

2. Lorne Sanny suggests that there are three major tasks of the church of Jesus Christ. What are they and how do they relate to caring?

3. In this chapter ten principles of the caring church were discussed. What principles are present in your church? What can be done about developing ones that are not seen much in your church? How can you personally assist in this development?

4. Romans 12:1 states that we worship God by offering our bodies as living and holy sacrifices. What does this mean in a practical sense? In what ways can you worship God? Be specific. How do worship and caring relate?

Chapter 4

1. The author describes Joni Eareckson's accident and questions why things like this happen. Have you ever experienced tragedy in your life or shared in a friend's tragedy? Did you ask "why?" How did you answer? How have you responded to those who have met tragedy in their lives? Would there have been a more effective way for you to respond? How?

2. Discussed in this chapter are four reasons for suffering. What are they? Do you agree or disagree with any of these? If you disagree, what are your reasons? Can you think of any other reasons there may be for suffering? What are they?

3. The author suggests that as Christians we ought to expect suffering, especially because of our faith. What does "suffering for our faith" mean? In what ways could you suffer because of your faith? How have you suffered because of your faith? What could you or a fellow-believer do to prepare for possible suffering?

4. If you are suffering, what is your attitude toward your pain? Is there any good that can come out of your pain? What is it?

Chapter 5

1. In this chapter the author lists four assumptions about healing and caring. What are these assumptions? Why is it important to understand these?

2. In caring "we don't apply some magical formula to everyone," but we care by showing a deep concern for people. In what ways can this deep concern be expressed to others? Do you have any suggestions on caring for others that the author did not mention? What are these? How can you become a more caring person?

3. Several principles of caring are listed in this chapter. What are these principles? Which ones do you feel are already seen in your life? On which ones do you need more work? How could you develop these?

4. The biblical account of Job was used in this chapter to illustrate how not to care as well as how to care. What were some of the ways in which Job's friends were not caring? How did Elihu demonstrate to Job that he really cared about Job? Like Job's comforters, do you ever care more because of your needs than because of the needs of another? Is this bad? How could you change?

Chapter 6

1. This chapter states that "there is nothing wrong with recognizing our good points" and that "there is nothing spiritual about condemning ourselves." Do you agree or disagree? Why? Do you recognize your good points? How do you accept compliments from others? How can you work to overcome your weaknesses?

2. The author suggests ways in which we can improve our self-image. What are these? What can you do to change your self-image?

3. What are the characteristics of a mature individual? On which ones do you have to work? How do you plan to improve?

4. The author lists several ways in which we can prevent "burnout." What are these? Are you caring for yourself? If not, how will you do this? How does this list help us to care for others?

Chapter 7

1. This chapter is introduced by discussing the characteristics of a truly religious person. What are these? What would you add to the author's list?

2. The author suggests that the Bible places people in three categories. Describe each of these. In which category are you? In what categories are your family and friends? How do you influence your friends and family spiritually? How do they influence you?

3. Many of us like to blame others for our problems and conflicts whether they are at fault or not. Why do you think we do this? In the past how have you handled conflicts with others? How could you handle conflicts in a better way? When others are at fault, how could we deal with the situation?

4. Counselors state that a major cause for conflict between people is faulty communication. How can we be more effective in our communication? What is your weakest area in communicating? What could you do to become a better communicator? Be specific.

5. Look at the quote by Francis Schaeffer. Do you agree? Does this influence the way you care? How could you change?

Chapter 8

1. In this chapter the author suggests several reasons why families have problems. What are some of these reasons? Would you add others? Which of these issues do you struggle with in your family? How could other caring people help you?

2. Do you find it easier to care for others than it is to care for your own family? If so, what are the reasons for this? What could you do to care more for your family? Be specific.

3. Read the quote by Dr. Gene Getz. Have you ever thought of your family as a miniature church? What does this suggest concerning your responsibilities to your family? What could be changed in your family to make it more like the church? Be specific.

4. Is your family one that reaches out to others? If not, what prevents your family from doing this? In what ways can your family begin to care for others more effectively? What goals do you have for your family?

Chapter 9

1. Do you agree with the author that we should be concerned about people in our communities? How do you care for those in your community now and how can you become more caring?

2. The author lists three decisions that must be made before we get involved in acts of caring, What are these? How can they apply to the way in which you care?

3. Have you ever experienced a crisis personally? How did others care for you? How have you helped others face a crisis? Do you think the ABC approach would be useful in helping people handle crises? What other things can we do to help in a crisis? Can we prepare ourselves for personal crises which may come in the future? Try to be specific.

4. As individuals can we do anything about the problems in the world and in our communities? What does the author suggest about this? What would you add? Do you agree that pointing individuals to Jesus Christ will help the world? How can you point others to Jesus Christ in your everyday activities?

Chapter 10

1. In this chapter the author writes about visiting speakers and musicians. Have you ever thought that these people have struggles just like the rest of us? In what practical ways could you care for a visitor who may be leading a seminar, speaking, or presenting special music in your church?

2. What are some of the pressures of the ministry as suggested by Dr. Briscoe? Do you think your pastor is experiencing any of these? Which ones? Are *you* creating any of these stresses? How could you care for your pastor more effectively? Be specific.

3. The author writes, "The church leader's responsibility is not to do all the work while everybody else sits back and watches." What is your attitude toward your church leaders? Have you even thought about how your gifts could be used in your church body? In what specific ways could you further the ministry of your church?

4. How could you be more caring of your community leaders? Does caring for community leaders mean that you must agree with their positions on political or other issues? How can you care even if you disagree with the leader's ideas? Would you add anything to the author's suggestions?

Chapter 11

1. In this chapter the author suggests that people often have doubts concerning God and spiritual issues. How have you dealt with your

doubts? How did Jesus handle doubters? Does this say anything about how we should handle the doubts which may arise in ourselves or others?

2. Os Guinness gives a number of causes for doubt. What are these? Which ones were the causes for your doubt? Does the list by Guinness help you in caring for others who have doubts?

3. This chapter contains a method for caring about those who doubt. What is this method? Can you think of anything to add to this method? What would you add?

4. It seems that some people do not want to believe no matter how much you care and no matter what the evidence. What is your reaction to a person like this? How can you care for a person who remains a doubter (and seems to enjoy this)?

Chapter 12

1. In this chapter the author suggests that Christians may still have personal struggles even though we are God's children. Is this true for you? If not, what has enabled you to avoid these struggles? If you are struggling, how has your commitment to Christ enabled you to handle your everyday struggles in more effective ways?

2. It is suggested in this chapter that we handle our stresses and hurts in different ways. What are some of these ways? How do you handle your stresses? Do you think there is a more effective way to handle your stresses and hurts? What makes it difficult to receive help from others when you are hurting?

3. What does the author say are some of the causes of loneliness? How should people who are lonely deal with their loneliness? What could you do if a lonely person came to you looking for comfort and help?

4. Each one of us has been worried or anxious at some time in life. How have your worries and anxieties affected you? How did you deal with them? Are there suggestions in this chapter that could help you to deal with these feelings in yourself or others? What are these suggestions?

5. There are a number of causes for depression stated in this chapter. What are these causes? Which ones have applied to you? In your own life, how have you dealt with discouragement? How could you care for others when they are discouraged?

Chapter 13

1. Although anger is not always wrong, it can be harmful. Describe some of the ways in which anger can be harmful. When is anger not harmful and not sinful? Describe a time when you expressed harmful anger and a time when you expressed "righteous anger." What happened after you expressed this anger?

2. How can we control our anger? Have you ever tried some of the suggestions presented in this chapter? How did things turn out?

3. Forgiveness is important in the healing process. We learn to forgive others by learning first to forgive ourselves. Have you forgiven yourself for things done in the past? If not, why not? Could your lack of self-forgiveness hinder your ability to forgive others? What could you do to help others forgive themselves and forgive others?

4. What are the major pressures in your life? How have you handled these pressures? How could you handle pressures in a more effective way? How can we really care for those who are under a lot of pressure?

Chapter 14

1. What kinds of losses have you experienced in your life? How did you handle these losses? How did others care for you in your loss? Do you think that going through a loss can help you to care more effectively for others who face similar circumstances? How can you care for others in times of loss?

2. Read the quotation by Chaplain Bittner. Have you ever thought of illness in this way? Do you agree or disagree with the quotation? Why? Have you ever benefited from an illness? How can you care for others who are ill?

3. What are the stages that most terminally ill patients go through? Have you ever thought about your own death and imagined yourself going through these stages? How can we prepare for death—our own, and that of loved ones? How can we care for others who are facing death?

4. The author suggests several ways in which we can learn to live a more productive and meaningful life. How can we help others care for us? How can we help our friends and family members to live more productive and meaningful lives?

Index